# Towards the Dawn

'When I was young, before I lost my eyesight,' Jamal had added, 'I wanted to write a symphony of these hills – the hills of God. I wanted to write about their glory and everlasting meaning. I wanted to write about the people who lived and still live on them. I wanted to write about their deaths, for here a divine human conquered death with death.'

Ibrahim Fawal, *On the Hills of God*
(NewSouth Books, 2002)

# Towards the Dawn

## A Journey through
## Easter to Pentecost

Garth Hewitt

First published in Great Britain in 2004 by
Society for Promoting Christian Knowledge
Holy Trinity Church
Marylebone Road
London NW1 4DU

British Library Cataloguing-in-Publication Data

A catalogue record for this book is available
from the British Library

ISBN 0-281-05591-2

1 3 5 7 9 10 8 6 4 2

Typeset by Avocet Typeset, Chilton, Aylesbury, Bucks
Printed in Great Britain by Bookmarque Ltd, Croydon, Surrey

# CONTENTS

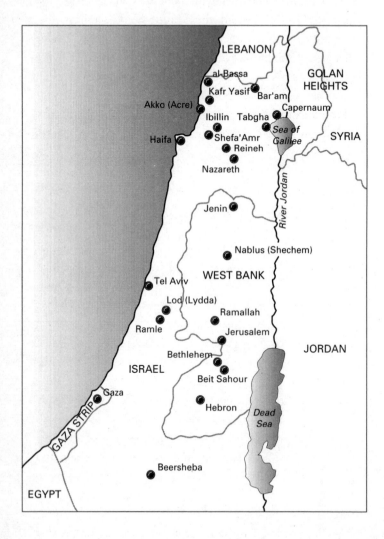

# FOREWORD

I have followed Garth Hewitt for many years since his first visit to Galilee. Behind the beautiful voice I have discovered something much stronger than the singer. I have discovered a man who believes in the dignity of every person and who because of his faith in God never gives up his belief in his fellow human beings. Our students at Mar Elias Educational Institution have sung his songs, and they have been danced and celebrated. His fine spirit resonates with the joy and suffering of marginalized peoples and groups. He can sing to them, 'Stronger than the Storm'. He can call them 'Children of Abraham'. He can humble himself and join them praying in the bosom of the earth in 'Abuna's Grotto'. What makes him special is his authentic concern for the well-being of the Jews in Israel together with his very deep, sincere sympathy with the Palestinian suffering. He has seen beyond the 'Writings on the Walls', beyond the slogans, and deeper than the whispers. He has seen people denied their human right and his is a strong voice, shouting not in the desert, but in the populated streets of our towns and villages: prepare the way for the Lord!

I know how seriously he wanted to visit the holy shrines, the antiquities, in order to go beyond these and to live as long as he could with the 'living stones' of the Holy Land, his Christian brothers and sisters. It is in them and through them that he tried to discover what remains in their lives of the real Man of Galilee. He created bonds of friendship with Palestinian Arab Christians. He is at home with them, and at the same time he has never omitted or neglected his important relationships with his Jewish friends. He is the one about whom we can easily say: *He took sides but never accepted to become one-sided.*

This present writing, that includes a touch of politics with an expression of faith and a vision of hope, is of unique importance for three reasons. First, it is to get to know Garth Hewitt better. Second, it is to feel his concern for the well-being of both Jews and Palestinians. Finally, to issue a call for Western Christianity to get up, move, go ahead and show real, concrete solidarity with those Palestinian Christians who are still living in the Holy Land. Here Christian survival is threatened by ongoing intensive immigration, and soon the land of Jesus will be left without the community that was commissioned to witness the importance of love, even for the enemy, of compassion, even for the persecutor, and of forgiveness for and from the two sides of the conflict.

I have the great pleasure to introduce Garth Hewitt's attempt to describe what is in his soul and how, in the geographical places, his eyes see Palestinian Christians' perseverance in survival, and the privilege that these Christians have amidst their sufferings, to go forward laden with the mission of their Compatriot, the Man of Galilee, Jesus Christ. They are to give hope where hope has been destroyed and a smile where tears have abounded, and to hold hands together where hands have been used to pull the trigger to kill each other.

This message is important. This vision is vital. What will you, my dear friend and reader, do with it? This is not a book to be read and put aside. This is a work to get to know to further your own commitment, maybe your own conversion and surely your own faith. In a future based on justice that radiates peace for Jews and Palestinians,

Christians and non-Christians can then spread hope for other nations, who base their security on military might that achieves nothing but fear. May Garth Hewitt be blessed for his courage to speak the truth, to call for integrity, and to live his faith as a role model for us all.

Abuna Elias Chacour
Ibillin
August 2003

# INTRODUCTION

St Jerome said that the Holy Land is the Fifth Gospel, and a journey there in the company of local Christians or 'living stones' opens one's eyes in a special way to this extraordinary gospel story and its relevance to today.

Having written a Lent book on Jerusalem (*Pilgrims and Peacemakers*), and an Advent book on Bethlehem (*Candle of Hope*), I felt I should do one on Nazareth and Galilee, and make it a journey from Easter to Trinity Sunday.

The book is divided into daily readings with most days beginning with a Bible passage. It is written in a devotional context and at the end of each chapter there is a prayer and, sometimes, a suggestion of how we might respond. The book visits holy sites that relate to the time of year – Easter, St George's Day, Ascension, Pentecost and Trinity – but also spends time in Nazareth and Galilee, and a few days in the Bethlehem area, and in each situation there are comments from local Christians, Jews or Muslims, to increase our knowledge and understanding of how faith and peacemaking are being worked out there.

When I first wrote the other books I assumed they would soon be out of date because the road to peace would have progressed. Sadly this has not been the case. Once again my hope and prayer would be that peace with justice and security for both Palestinian and Israeli will become a reality. At the moment it looks as though the way to peace will be long and difficult; that is why this book is called *Towards the Dawn*. This seems to be the darkest hour, yet we know that the darkest hour comes just before the dawn and in the book the hope of resurrection is never far away.

I interviewed Christians, Jews and Muslims for the book. Some of these people appeared in my previous books but some are new; they all represent a cast of extraordinary characters who attempt to live and witness to peacemaking in the middle of one of the most painful situations in the world. In their very lives they are walking towards the dawn and they give us hope and an example as to how to do the same.

The book is a journey to Nazareth and Galilee, and the Christian community there is predominantly from the indigenous population, with roots going back in this land long before 1948. They are therefore Israeli Palestinians or Arabs, and part of the 20 per cent of Israeli citizens in this category. Their situation, rarely publicized, comes to light in this book; they feel forgotten and many, having been made refugees in 1948 or soon after, fear it could happen again; they need our support and understanding at this time.

I would like to thank all the people that I interviewed who were so helpful. I do not have space for everything they said but they gave me the story to tell – their names are in the book.

Special thanks to all at Amos Trust for giving me the time to do this book and also helping me with it. It very much reflects Amos Trust's ongoing commitment to a spirituality and a way of life that supports and works with peacemakers on the road to justice and wholeness for all. Thanks to Sue and Simon Plater and Clare Dowding (who joined me on the journey and helped with transcribing interviews), Gill King (transcribing interviews – a third time!), and to Wisam Salsaa, Khalil Harouny and Rimon Maklouf (my guides).

And finally to my companion, Gill, who loses me for a month or two when I write these books!

My hope is renewed and refreshed by these peace-makers who accompany us on this journey but my spirit is very disturbed at what I saw and heard. Now is the time to listen to them and then speak up – the call comes loud and clear: there is 'naught for your comfort' once again in this beautiful land we once called 'Holy'.

Garth Hewitt
All Hallows on the Wall
August 2003

# WEEK 1: TRIUMPH OF ANOTHER WAY

## Easter Sunday: 'Look, there is the place they laid him . . .'

Mark 16.1–7
Very early on the first day of the week . . . they entered the tomb, they saw a young man . . . and they were alarmed. But he said to them, 'Do not be alarmed; you are looking for Jesus of Nazareth, who was crucified. He has been raised; he is not here. Look, there is the place they laid him. But go, tell his disciples and Peter that he is going ahead of you to Galilee; there you will see him, just as he told you.'

Our journey from Easter to Trinity begins at the Church of the Resurrection (or the Church of the Holy Sepulchre), which explodes with light and fire at Easter with the ceremony of Holy Fire. Pushing, shoving, even fighting can all be part of it. Often when I have been in the church (though never at Easter), it has been very crowded, and at first I found it hard to understand the building. Now I have been more often and the last couple of times there have, sadly, been very few people.

Actually it is two buildings with the middle covered in for security at some stage. Stand outside at first, and look to the right-hand side of the church door – this is Calvary or the hill of Golgotha. Here in the early days of the Christian community, before this church was built, Confirmation candidates would spend the night on the eve of their Confirmation on the hill of Golgotha. It was built by St Helena, who destroyed the pagan temple that had previously been built to hide this site. The church is shared by the Orthodox, the Armenians and the Latins (Romans), then Copts, Syrians and Ethiopians each have a smaller portion, and even Anglicans have a special place for prayer under the bell on the balcony!

Inside the door to the left is what traditionally has been considered the tomb of Christ. Having had a look, go beyond it into a small room or cave which has a rock tomb, and this gives a better idea of what it may have been like; here one can imagine the shock and bewilderment of the women on that first Easter. The Garden Tomb on the Nablus Road is another place to go to ponder and be quiet; though it is too old a tomb to have been that of Jesus, it is a good place for thinking and meditation.

Why is it important to ponder these things? Because here in Jerusalem the Church was born. Thinking on these events, the early Church came to the conclusions we find in the Gospels about the character of Jesus.

'Look, there is the place they laid him . . . but . . . he is going ahead of you to Galilee . . .' In this book we will head on up to Galilee, and we are not on this journey simply to look only at traditional sites, but to see them through the eyes of today's church community who live here in the Holy Land, and have lived here, they are proud to say, since Pentecost. With them we shall go from Easter to Pentecost and Trinity. Yet this Church is predominantly Palestinian, which brings an added poignancy to the message of the gospel as we hear it from a Church that lives as part of a suffering community. We will also hear from peacemakers from both Jewish and Muslim communities, and discover how much all have in common as human beings on a journey to community and peace-making. (The Christians we meet in this chapter are mainly Palestinians who are also Israeli citizens, often known as Israeli Arabs.)

### 'We are still here'

For the local Church the experience of their sufferings means they do not separate the Good Friday experience from the Resurrection. I asked Bishop Riah Abu El-Assal, the Anglican Bishop in Jerusalem, how they view Easter, particularly in these difficult times:

'Here we continue walking through the Via Dolorosa, even today. Regardless of the fact that we are the community of the risen Lord, or the Resurrection, the daily experience of our people, in Jerusalem and Bethlehem and Ramallah and Nablus and Gaza, is the experience of our Lord carrying his cross and being unable to carry on with it, and we need someone like Simon of Cyrene to come and give us a hand with it. We continue to look for someone like Simon, but Simon is not to be found . . . So we continue to look to our sisters and brothers in Christ in Europe and the United States, and different parts of the world, who claim to be members of the One Body of Christ, to come and help carry the cross, even if it means paying a price. Simon of Cyrene knew that carrying the cross to Golgotha meant that Christ would be hanged on it. But he realized that if it was not for Golgotha there would be no Resurrection; without death there is no Resurrection. Our people have experienced that over the years, but they also experienced the Resurrection in many ways; every time the Israelis say, "We're done, we've done it, we're finished with them," it is strange how we rise again. We rise to our feet and challenge the authorities: *we are still here*.'

## 'The dawn of the resurrection which starts and never ends'

Bishop Riah is a man from Nazareth, and his story is told in the book *Caught in Between* (SPCK, 1999). Also from Galilee, and living not far from Nazareth in Ibillin, comes Abuna Elias Chacour, whose book *Blood Brothers* (Chosen Books, 1984, reprinted 2003) has also opened people's eyes to the years of struggle for the Palestinian people. When I visited him one lunchtime up in Ibillin, he said of Easter:

'For us Easter starts 40 days before the Resurrection; it is a procession towards the Resurrection. Every evening Christians gather in the churches to pray, preparing the celebration of the Resurrection, and it culminates in three points: Palm Sunday; Good Friday (which we call Sad Friday), when Christ is crucified – but then we sing "although you are on the cross, show us your Resurrection", because we are aware that Good Friday is a period of 24 hours, and it will be succeeded by the dawn of the Resurrection, which starts and never ends . . . and the culmination of the Resurrection would be, not the Ascension, but the day of Pentecost, when we receive the Holy Spirit, when we receive the wind of God. The wind of God was a strong wind that you call in the West a storm. We were "stormed" with the Spirit of God, and he took all the bad ideas, all the previous ideas, all the prejudices, and made us understand that for those who believe in him, there is no more privilege for man against woman, lord against slave, no more privilege for Jew against Gentile. That's easily acceptable today; but what if I say there is no privilege for Jew against Palestinian? On that day of Pentecost, we were born as believers in Christ. Who are "we"? Greeks, Romans, Jews, Gentiles and Arabs – all of them composing one community, the community of God, the community of the new believers, those who believe that everyone who was created as a baby is created in the image of the likeness of God, and is invited to the divine banquet. It is not special people who are invited – everybody is invited, so be ready to listen to the whispers of God who knocks on your door. Come on your own – you are invited, and it's up to you to answer, "Yes, Lord, speak – I'm here." Or maybe it's too noisy inside you, you have too many weapons, too much money, you don't have time to listen to the whispers, and the Lord passes by.'

## Monday: In the Upper Room

John 20.19–23
When it was evening on that day, the first day of the week, and the doors of the house where the disciples had met were locked for fear ... Jesus came and stood among them ...

The Upper Room, known as the Cenacle, is on Mount Zion (the name given by the Byzantines to the hill outside Zion Gate in the south-west corner of the Old City; David's Zion never extended this far, but the name has stuck). This room was not there in the time of Jesus, but was built later and was part of the abbey and church called Holy Sion, Mother of All Churches. The church was built to commemorate the events that happened in the Upper Room, and in the room one can see Crusader work commemorating the Last Supper and Pentecost. In 1552 the room was adapted for Muslim worship; there is a Muslim *mihrab* or prayer niche on one wall.

Though this is a beautiful room, it is probably more rewarding and mysterious to go to another Upper Room, in the Syrian Orthodox Convent of St Mark, in the Armenian Quarter. Our guide, Rimon, was keen for us to visit here, and though it is a little hidden away it was a fascinating and very worthwhile experience.

## Downstairs to the Upper Room

An Iraqi sister explained to us that this was the first Christian church, the mother church of Christianity, and can be dated to 37 AD – this certainly made me sit up! She then explained that it was the house of Mary the mother of Mark; it was the place of the Last Supper, and St James the brother of Jesus used to live here. It was also here that Peter came when he was released from prison (the story's told in Acts 12). There is a famous icon here reputed to have been painted by St Luke in 50 AD (it is in fact very old but probably not pre-Byzantine).

The Syrian Orthodox church is ancient and fascinating, and the sister talking to us was a passionate evangelist; she had been most concerned that a previous visitor was not a believer. The most interesting aspect of the church is that their liturgy is in Aramaic, the language of Jesus and a living language in the part of Iraq from which the sister comes. In 1940 an Aramaic inscription was found in the church dating back to the fifth or sixth century which seems to support the ancient claims of the church. One can get cynical or even blasé about sites in the Holy Land, but as usual one has to recognize that it is not the authenticity that is all-important but the lessons learnt from the place.

The sister told us that this had been a place of healing, even in recent times. After lighting candles, she told us she was going to take us 'downstairs to the Upper Room'. It sounded a curious anomaly but of course was technically accurate, accounting for the changing levels of Jerusalem. Here, in a not especially impressive room, the unexpected hit me. She stood by the altar and sang the Lord's Prayer in Aramaic. Rimon began to sing along gently and the years seemed to roll away – they seemed to touch Jesus. I looked from one to the other – such utter sincerity. The Upper Room seemed to contain a motley collection of things but all this disappeared – their voices together sounded healing, and it took me into the past, thinking of all that happened in this area of Jerusalem; somewhere near this spot the roots of our faith found birth, something happened to unlock the doors that were closed by fear, and these Middle Eastern Christians open doors for visiting pilgrims to remind us of the importance of the heritage of our faith. Here the 'Fifth Gospel' comes alive. In return for what they show us we must not forget them.

We leave the Syriac church and go on to St James' Armenian Cathedral which is nearby, not too far from the Jaffa Gate. I had timed it so we could attend their liturgy, which begins daily at 3.30 p.m. It is a wonderful experience and well worth including as part of your pilgrimage in Jerusalem. There are paintings and icons on the walls of the cathedral, and there was a mystical atmosphere, a feeling of touching ancient roots. We had moved from Aramaic to Armenian, and again there was a real sense of holiness and sacred space.

Both churches are good to visit to bring our faith into perspective. There is a remarkable history and heritage, and to take part in liturgies that have not changed for centuries has a sobering effect. It reminded me of the words of John Meier, that 'nothing ages faster than relevance' (*A Marginal Jew: Rethinking the Historical Jesus*, vol. 2, Doubleday, 1994). These places of worship are not interested in relevance, and consequently they can speak to our world in a most significant way. The hunger for relevance may have left the Church strangely bereft.

*Prayer*

> Speak, O God, through the echoes of the centuries, of a story that holds the key for how we live now. And keep us mindful of those who have kept the torch of witness alight. May our lives show that we have moved from our Upper Room of fear to be those who carry your light of hope and resurrection into a world of need. Amen.

## Tuesday: Light in the midst of darkness

John 20.24–29
'Unless I see . . . I will not believe.'

We are still in the Upper Room, and this is the passage that makes Thomas famous, somewhat unfairly, as 'doubting Thomas'. I say 'somewhat unfairly' because he is being asked to believe something very staggering, that he would no doubt love to believe, but frankly he is a realist.

Yaseed Said is one of the young clergy of the Anglican Diocese of Jerusalem; he comes from Kafr Yasif in Galilee.

He is currently working as acting Dean of St George's Cathedral in Jerusalem. His comments about the current situation are a bit Thomas-like; he would love to believe that the 'road map' to peace will work, but he is also a realist because of all he has seen in the past. However, his resurrection faith does mean that he has not lost hope.

## The light of Christ in the midst of death

He says: 'The situation on the ground is very difficult. There have been talks that could lead to something better, but my perception of things is that the road map is not really going to make a great difference. I think that if Palestinian people were important to the world, then the world would have done something a long time ago; this has been going on for over 50 years now, and it's quite obvious that what's happening to the people of this land is not significant. So you can say I am pessimistic, but don't think that I don't have hope, because I make the distinction between hope and optimism; I think that if you are hopeful it doesn't necessarily mean that you think things will be better the following month, or in a few months; it means that you can see light – not replacing darkness, but you can see light even in the midst of darkness, which is how I come to see the story of Christ. And that's how I come to see his Resurrection; it doesn't come as a negation – Good Friday is still there.

'We are trying to learn how to celebrate Easter in the midst of Good Friday. Think about the history of this city; Jerusalem has always been a place of death, suffering and conflict, and hopelessness. But we still call it a holy city, where holiness doesn't necessarily happen to appear very clearly. But I think the Easter story gives us a different perspective on holiness. I think holiness in the perspective of Easter is not about healthy mentality or flawless relationships; it is about how to acknowledge the grace of God in the midst of all the disorder, and it's about how to see the light of Christ in the midst of all the death. It's about how to see the commitment and the faithfulness of God's vulnerability in the midst of this chaos. So the Resurrection of Jesus has not cancelled out our problems, but it has shown us that in the midst of total and utter darkness there comes hope, which is the source of survival and resilience in the midst of all this.'

So back to doubting Thomas: his story seems to have been one of remarkable faith. Once he had seen and believed, his response 'My Lord and my God' seems to have been one of the most deeply felt responses. 'Ironically,' says Herman D'Souza, 'it was the doubting apostle's Easter joy which turned out to be the greatest' (*In the Steps of St Thomas*, Madras-Mylapore: Diocesan Press, 1983). After Pentecost he heads east to found the Church in India; the legacy of this remarkable journey is the Indian Church of today.

## Wednesday: Healing the wounds of the Holy Land

Psalm 82.1–4, 8
Give justice to the weak and the orphan; maintain the right of the lowly and the destitute. Rescue the weak and needy; deliver them from the hand of the wicked ... Rise up, O God ... for all the nations belong to you!

St George's Hostel is a great place to stay in Jerusalem. It is in the compound of the Cathedral Church of St George the Martyr. It is an oasis of peace with a beautiful garden where you can sit and meet people, drink mint tea and relax. The cathedral is the mother church of the Diocese of Jerusalem, and is home to two congregations: the indigenous Palestinian Anglicans for whom this place is their parish church, whose 9.30 Sunday service is in Arabic; and also the expatriate members of the community, pilgrims and tourists who come here to worship, and for them the 11.00 service is in English.

The cathedral was built at the end of the nineteenth century on the Nablus Road, not far from the Damascus Gate and the Garden Tomb. The cathedral is sensitively decorated with local Palestinian handiwork. At the back there are two fonts – the conventional Western one given by Queen Victoria, as well as one for total immersion installed in 1905, which was built to reassure the Eastern Churches, who practise full immersion, of the orthodoxy of Anglican baptism. The advantage of staying at the hostel is the opportunity to take part in the daily worship in the cathedral.

## Holistic approach to peacemaking

Near the beginning of my trip, I received a phone call from Yehezkel Landau; he and his wife Dalia have been featured in both my previous books. Along with Michail Fanous, they run Open House, a reconciliation centre based in Ramle in Israel. The phone call was inspiring, as usual, and because Yehezkel was leaving the next day for the USA he sent me some articles to show me some of his recent thinking.

Yehezkel, of course, is Jewish, but he believes that there

should be an alliance of Christians, Muslims and Jews for healing the wounds of the Holy Land. He believes that one of the reasons the Oslo peace process failed was that there was 'a "congenital defect" in the Oslo concept: its rationalist assumption of how the conflict could be resolved. The negotiators were secular nationalists who tried to impose a "secular" peace plan on a Holy Land whose inhabitants include many people motivated by religious passions.'

Yehezkel calls for 'a more holistic approach to peacemaking' which would include 'a different understanding of holiness . . . to be taught by religious leaders and educators. Jews, Christians, Muslims, Druze and others in the Holy Land are hungry for an experience of true holiness, based in an awareness of the all-loving and inclusively just God. Partisan interpretations of the sacred, especially regarding territory and history, need to be supplanted by a different theological paradigm whose essence can be summarized as "pluralistic monotheism".'

### 'The land belongs to God alone'

'The one true God not only suffers or tolerates difference; that God has created individuals and nations with such striking differences in order to create a variegated human community that can celebrate diversity instead of feeling threatened by it. If both Jews and Palestinians can be brought to see, and to know deeply, that the land belongs to God alone, and that by the grace of God both peoples belong to the land (see Exodus 19.5–6), then a new political vision can be generated on this spiritual foundation . . .

'For this to happen, religious educators have to assume responsibility for developing and teaching an inclusive understanding of holiness. Without a shared spiritual commitment to genuine sacrifice – humility and renunciation for the sake of God – all the peace plans advanced by diplomats will fail ... God's Holy Land is meant to be a laboratory for practising justice and compassion towards all. As privileged inhabitants of the land, we are called to transcend the bloody, divisive past and create a common future. If we rise to the challenge, we will all be blessed by the holiness of Shalom, Salaam, Peace. And then life will prevail, not death and destruction' ('A Holistic Peace Process for the Middle East', quoted in *How Long O Lord?*, ed. Maurine and Robert Tobin, Cowley Publications, 2002).

To me, it is wonderful that Yehezkel has not lost his vision and his hope, nor his sense that religion still has a part to play. Sometimes when I hear the bitterness and bigotry in the name of religion I think it is only the secularists that can save us from ourselves. Yehezkel's call is, in a way, the last chance for the religious to show we are not for ever bound by primitive and tribal views of God that have so dominated and spoilt this part of the world; that there is a way forward that reveals the inclusive, compassionate God that Yehezkel talks about. In the darkest hour Yehezkel can still see a God of hope and so a vision of hope.

## Thursday: Injustice will not have the last word

John 20.29
Jesus said to him, 'Have you believed because you have seen me? Blessed are those who have not seen and yet have come to believe.'

13

The Revd Dr Naim Ateek is President of the Sabeel Centre in Jerusalem, an ecumenical grassroots liberation theology movement among Palestinian Christians, born out of the pastoral need of how to find a liberating gospel when some people use the Bible to oppress them. A visit to Sabeel should not be missed; it is only just down the road from St George's Cathedral, so one morning we headed down the road to meet Naim and to ask him first about Easter.

## God's final word is for life

'For me, Easter has always been a very significant feast, because the Easter message has always been a message of triumph and victory over sin, over death, over injustice, over evil, and it is the final word of God. God did not allow the final word to be the human word of crucifixion and death, and evil victorious over good and the innocent. Because Good Friday stood for what seems to be the triumph of evil: evil and people in power can place the innocent on the cross, they can condemn the innocent; here, in this case, political power and religious power binding together and placing Christ on the cross. And that seems to be the final statement: we are able to do what we want and we can kill, we can put you on the cross.

'Yet Easter comes to say, "Sorry, that's not the way it's going to be," because God's final word is for life, for victory for justice, for resurrection, not for death, not for evil. And so our message for Easter has always been – all the Church, loud and clear – that we believe in the victory of God in the resurrection of Christ. And when I translate it to the political realm, I believe that it is this Easter message that says that evil and injustice will not have the last word, and we live in the hope of the resurrection, in the hope of life, in the hope of joy and liberation, and that ultimately is what is going to happen. For people who have been experiencing so much injustice and so much oppression, by the power of God and because of God's justice they will ultimately experience a new life, and a new life in this country, and hopefully also a new reconciliation between people. So the theology of Easter is very crucial, and then translating it into people's experience of everyday life, especially people who are living under occupation and oppression.'

## Resurrection in Pasadena

Resurrection is such a powerful concept; as Naim is saying, it reminds us that injustice does not have the last word – and death does not have the last word. An incident that happened when my wife, Gill, and I visited the Church of All Saints', Pasadena, in California, reminded me powerfully of this. It was All Saints' Day and the service was deeply moving in a quiet, ordered way. People were there to mourn the loved ones they had lost, particularly in the last year, and to commend these loved ones to God. The theme of the service was a celebration of life in the presence of death, and many tears were shed. One woman particularly caught my eye; she was the other side of the aisle and a little further up the church, and she was distraught with grief. At one point the choir processed down into the congregation, singing the hymn 'For All the Saints'. As they went past the weeping woman, one of the choir hugged her, with that informality linked with ritual that is so well done in the Episcopal Church in the United States; it was touching to see. The choir moved on, leading the congregation in the singing of the hymn and then heading back to the sanctuary.

Then an extraordinary thing happened. As the choir went up the chancel step, there was a musical break, featuring the orchestra, that led into the last two verses of the hymn, and it was stunning as we soared into 'But lo, there breaks a yet more glorious day', and everyone sang the last two verses with such power and such hope, as if their lives depended on it – and maybe they did.

I looked across the aisle, and a wonderful thing had happened: the weeping woman was still weeping, but now she was upright, her head was back, and she was singing with all her might, against all the pain and hurt. As the tears still streamed down her face, she sang, 'The saints triumphant rise in bright array . . . Alleluia, alleluia.'

It was resurrection against all the odds – such faith – and now tears came down my face, because of the witness of this grieving woman, who with such determination held on to resurrection and faith, 'Singing to Father, Son and Holy Ghost: Alleluia, alleluia.'

In this beautiful service we were made conscious of the sacred and the holy, our spirits were lifted, but the sermon had addressed down-to-earth issues of justice, compassion and inclusivity. The service lifted people up to the higher values, to the character of a holy, sacred God who includes all and who touches all the painful issues of everyday life. Resurrection hope came through struggle, and became a tangible reality in the worship on that Sunday morning.

The Easter message is needed in the pain of Palestine and in the personal struggles of Pasadena. It is the same principle: 'God does not allow the final word . . . to be crucifixion and death . . . God's final word is for life . . . justice and resurrection.'

# Friday: Seeing in the light of the risen Christ

Matthew 28.5–20
'. . . he is going ahead of you to Galilee; there you will see him' . . . Now the eleven disciples went to Galilee, to the mountain to which Jesus had directed them. When they saw him, they worshipped him; but some doubted . . . 'Remember, I am with you always . . .'

It is time to head up to Galilee to hear from the people there, and to pause as pilgrims and let our spirits be renewed. As Mark 16.7 says, 'he is going ahead of you to Galilee . . .' The disciples had to return to where they were from, and for us as pilgrims we are inspired in order to return and live out the gospel in our situation with better understanding and with renewed vision.

We will visit Nazareth (Jesus' home town) and Capernaum, where Jesus lived as he carried out his Galilee ministry. We will meet local Christians from the towns and villages of Galilee, and learn from them while discovering their situation. One of the churches of Galilee that we will visit is St Paul's Episcopal Church in the town of Shefa'Amr. The vicar is Fuad Dagher, a young priest whom I have known for years, since he was in the youth group at Christ Church, Nazareth. I asked him for his thoughts on Easter.

*'We are in the Upper Room . . .'*
'Easter is *the* feast of the East, and I think we have so much to tell the world because it has to do with the East.

Having in mind the whole journey of our Lord Jesus Christ from the beginning of Holy Week until the end, we as Palestinians find the scene is repeating itself in our story – this scene of crucifixion, of terrorism against Christ, of disciples gathered in the room in fear, and when Jesus appeared to them, the first thing he said was, "My peace I give to you, my peace I leave with you." We are in this Upper Room in one way or another, Ramallah, Zababdeh, Jenin, the whole West Bank is the Upper Room; where Palestinians are inside the room, closing their doors in fear. The Palestinians will get their full rights and justice and reconciliation will come; the Palestinians will rise again with their own right to live freely, with their own state, side by side with the State of Israel.'

Fuad then talked about the Anglican Church in the Diocese of Jerusalem, which he feels has a very hopeful future:

'I am very proud of our Church: our Church is witnessing a resurrection, our Church is witnessing hope, with good numbers of young clergy, and young people in the Church, who are the present leaders as well as the future. They keep talking about us as the future of the Church, but we are also the present; we are what we are now, not only what we are going to be. We are the present and the future ready to continue the walk and the talk, and to carry on this life and to pass it on to future generations.'

## Going back to where they started

And we hear from Yaseed Said again:

'One of the things to note in the story of the Resurrection, especially in John's Gospel, is the apparition stories; all these stories are about going back to where they started, sticking to their origins, acknowledging that, accepting it, with its past, with all its wounds, with all its difficulties, but seeing it in a totally different light, which is the light of the risen Christ. And that's something that happens on the shores of Tiberias; Peter comes to meet Christ again when he decides to go and start fishing again. So that's where those narratives come very powerfully alive to the peoples of this land today; it's how to stick to your origins, how to relate to your background, how to not deny your story and your roots. Healing only comes when you go back to them and say, "This is what happened, and this is where I am, this is where I've been, this is what I've done, this is how I go on." So accepting that reality is really the secret for conquering it, and getting over it.'

## Saturday: Journey back to wholeness

John 21.1–24
After these things Jesus showed himself again to the disciples by the Sea of Tiberias ... Just after daybreak, Jesus stood on the beach; but the disciples did not know that it was Jesus ... He said to them, 'Cast the net to the right side of the boat ...' So they cast it, and now they were not able to haul it in because there were so many fish.

Thomas reacts with deep commitment after meeting with Jesus; now it is the turn of Peter. Once he has recognized who is standing on the shoreline he plunges in the water to get there quicker. They are all there, including Thomas, but there is still an air of uncertainty, a difficulty in recognizing the risen Jesus, even though, as the Gospel writer says, it is 'now the third time that Jesus appeared to the disciples after he was raised from the dead'. It is the occasion when Jesus asks Peter three times if he loves him and tells him to 'tend my sheep'. Peter, who denied him three times, has to go through this painful moment of penitence, but though hurt he says, 'Lord, you know everything; you know that I love you.' (This moment is commemorated by the Sea of Galilee at the Church of Mensa Christi, or Peter's Primacy – a little chapel by the lake surrounded by wonderful trees.)

Jesus does not seem to have been recognized at all when he told them to cast their net on the other side. It seems to be the fullness of the net that opens Peter's eyes. Everything in this passage is symbolic; it is 'just after daybreak', there is almost an air of despondency or of wondering what to do next – they 'have toiled all night and caught nothing' – and then the Resurrection breaks through. The darkest hour is just before dawn: it is that time when we might feel like giving up and then the call comes to 'cast your net again'. It is the journey back to wholeness; something breaks through our despair and says, 'There is hope, dawn is here.'

### Cast your net again

> Just at the point of giving up
> When the struggle had been so long
> On the downward slope of despair
> When everything seems so wrong
> Deep waters are around us

Bitter tears begin to fall
Take the time to be silent
Take time to hear the call

Cast your net again – it's not over
You'll find hope again – it's not over
Cast your net again – it's not over
Your life is not in vain – so cast your net again.

They say that the darkest hour
Is just before the dawn
But with the brand new day
Opportunities may come
You may have laboured all night
And the night has been very long
But you'll find that the darkest hour
Is just before the dawn

Cast your net again . . .

(Words and music Garth Hewitt
© Chain of Love Music)

At the end of this first week of Easter, the example of the Palestinian Church struggling towards the dawn in these dark days is a reminder to all of us to support them and pray for them and visit them. Their example is also a reminder to journey to hope ourselves, even when times are hard, to cast our nets again and find renewed vision in the light of the Risen One.

Take time this week to think what response you might make for the Church in Palestine and Israel. Take time to pray for them, to increase awareness and understanding, or if possible to visit the 'living stones' and hear their story first hand. Also remember to pray for Israeli and Palestinian – for Muslim, Jew and Christian and for those not from a faith community – that all may find renewed strength to walk the ways of justice and of peace.

*Prayer*

O God, our companion in this time of Easter, we ask that we will discover afresh the hope of the Resurrection. We are grateful for the Church that maintains its witness in the pains and struggles of Palestine and Israel. Thank you that even in these days of walking their Via Dolorosa they have not forgotten the Easter message that burst from the tomb in Jerusalem, spreading first around that land that once was holy, then reaching out to the whole world. Thank you that they have not let that flame die. May we not forget them and may our lives show the confidence of those who have also reached out and touched the living God, however tentatively and though we may have been filled with doubts. In our times of darkness, may we catch a glimpse of a flicker of light that reminds us that we are always walking towards the dawn as we walk with you, and may our hearts expand with hope as we sense the power and meaning of your resurrection. Amen.

# WEEK 2: THE SEARCH FOR ST GEORGE

## Sunday: The saint who conquered evil

Revelation 7.13–17
These are they who have come out of the great ordeal
... and the one who is seated on the throne will
shelter them. They will hunger no more, and thirst no
more; the sun will not strike them, nor any scorching
heat; for the Lamb at the centre of the throne will be
their shepherd, and he will guide them to springs of
the water of life, and God will wipe away every tear
from their eyes.

St George's Day comes on 23 April, soon after Easter.
George is patron saint of England, and yet his tomb is in
Lydda (now Lod near Tel Aviv). Many English people know
nothing of St George and few realize he was a Palestinian.
Bishop Riah went with President Arafat to visit Prime
Minister Tony Blair on one occasion, and the TV showed
them leaving 10 Downing Street; Bishop Riah was the last
one out, and he said something to Tony Blair. I asked him
later what he said, and he replied, 'I was reminding him that
his patron saint, St George, was a Palestinian!' On this trip
I felt it was time to find out about St George.

In Jerusalem the Anglican Cathedral is named after St
George. I spoke to Bishop Riah as we sat in the compound, and he said, 'I think the people of Lod will be able
to tell you more, because he is one of them. He is a

Palestinian from old Lydda. We celebrate because we are here at St George's Cathedral, and because he is a Palestinian saint we also try to remind the English people that he is not to be found in Canterbury but in Palestine. But we are happy they took him to be their patron saint; the way to honour him is to support his people, the Palestinians.'

My next interview was to take me even closer. I spoke to Susan and Samuel Barhoum up in Reineh in Galilee. Susan works for the Galilee Society, a Palestinian health and environmental agency, and Samuel is the Anglican vicar of both Holy Family Church in Reineh and Christ Church, Nazareth.

Susan reminded me: 'My father was born in Lydda [Audeh Rantisi, whose story is told in *Blessed are the Peacemakers*, Eagle Publishing, 2003], and Lydda is mentioned in Acts, where Simon Peter speaks to the people and they become Christians; they were some of the first Christians. My father's family can be traced back to the fourth century, when the church in Lydda was built; the church is St George's, and it was built by St Helena, who was the mother of Constantine. That was when records started, and they started recording births, priests and so on, in the church; my father's family were some of the first few priests in the church in the fourth century.'

Susan went on, 'The tomb of St George is there, and St George is most respected in Orthodox churches; he's the patron saint of most Orthodox churches in the country, because he was the one who killed the dragon or conquered evil. So he's very revered. On St George's Day they have a big celebration where people from all over the country go to Lydda, to the church, to celebrate St George. The story or fable says that there was this dragon that everybody was afraid of, and that anybody who ventured outside the village would be killed and eaten. St George was the person who came and had the courage to face the dragon, and was able to stab it and kill it; so that way he conquered evil and he killed the dragon, which was the sign of evil. I think England took St George from the Crusades, when they came here and they discovered St George and adopted him as their saint.'

Samuel commented that St George is a saint not only for Christians in the Holy Land but for Muslims and Jews as well.

## Monday: God has left this land

Revelation 3.15–22
To the one who conquers I will give a place with me on my throne, just as I myself conquered and sat down with my Father on his throne . . .

Now it was time to go to Lod to see the church where St George is buried. Lod used to be a wealthy Arab town before 1948, but now it is certainly not wealthy and it seems very run down. When the Arab population was driven out in 1948, military commander Moshe Dayan told the local Palestinian population to gather in the Dahamesh mosque and they would be safe. Hundreds went into the mosque but over 80 were gunned to death in there. Most of the rest were driven out of the town at gunpoint, like Audeh Rantisi (Susan's father), or fled.

The present church of St George was built just over a

25

hundred years ago on the ruins of the Crusader church, itself built over the Byzantine church of St Helena. The mosque next door, Jamia al-Omar, one of the oldest mosques in the region, is also built over part of the Byzantine church and is also dedicated to St George, who is known as Al-Khader in Arabic.

The church is not as striking as the church at the village of Al-Khader that we will visit later this week, but it has various icons of St George, and downstairs in the crypt is his tomb. Churches of St George were, and are, seen as places of healing, and indeed places of great power; many necklaces and rings had been left as gifts in thanks for healings.

We went to have lunch in a café down the road, where the owner came over to our table and told us that there would never be peace: 'Sharon is in one valley and Abu Mazen (Palestinian Prime Minister in June 2003) in the other and they are shouting at each another.' He then leaned over and told us, 'God has left this land.' At that moment he seemed depressingly right; it was only the faith of the people we met, the spirituality of the 'living stones', that showed us anything different.

But what about St George? Why is he patron saint of England? Our answer to this came in a meeting up in northern Galilee near the border with Lebanon. We were in a Christian village called Mi'ilya with an expert Arab historian, Shukri Arraf. He said that Richard the Lionheart beat Saladin in Lydda, in the late twelfth century, close to the St George/Al-Khader sanctuary. As a result of this, Richard the Lionheart was so impressed with St George that he brought him home to England. Clearly, the way all people of the Holy Land had such respect for George made him a figure to bring back and revere, and we were by no means the only ones who did this – the cult of St George had spread widely through the Christian East and Europe. Actually, St George was known in England prior to the Crusades, but maybe their experience raised his profile and was to lead to his significant role in England.

We saw yesterday how Susan Barhoum started to give us the clue as how to interpret the story of St George: the dragon represents evil, and George was prepared to stand up for what was right, and oppose evil. Tomorrow Elias Chacour will lead us further in this interpretation. Today, though, let's hear a little about the Church in Lod and nearby Ramle. Samuel Fanous is vicar of Emmanuel Episcopal Church in Ramle, and they also have a play centre very close to St George's in Lod, which was where I interviewed him. Sadly, since the last time I had been over his wife had died very suddenly, which was a deep trauma for him and the children. We chatted for a while about the family and how he was getting on, and then I asked him about church life in Ramle.

## Living ecumenically

'Our church is Emmanuel Episcopal, the other churches are Catholic and Orthodox. There are close to 4,000 Christians in Ramle. We have the Church of Arimathea, because Catholics think Ramle is Arimathea, where Joseph came from who buried Jesus. The Christian community is not a big community but we work ecumenically, and live ecumenically. When I was in seminary we took an ecumenical course; I looked at the professor and I thought, "Teacher, we live it, we don't study it." My sister is married to an Orthodox – she became an Orthodox. My father is an Anglican cantor; he likes the Evangelical tradition, singing and so on. I have one sister who is an Evangelical in Germany. The other sister is Orthodox in America. One of my uncles is Orthodox, another uncle is Catholic because his wife is Catholic. For people in Ramle, that's the way. They are married to each other. Any pastor or priest from different traditions who comes to Ramle cannot be other than open and tolerant and considerate. You have to accept everyone, and people come to our church even though they are not Anglicans. That's Christianity, living together in love and peace. So I'm not just talking ecumenism, we live it.'

## Tuesday: History, the myth and the meaning

Revelation 3.7–13
Look, I have set before you an open door, which no one is able to shut. I know that you have but little power, and yet you have kept my word and have not denied my name.

So I continued on my search for more information on St George. Any casual visitor to the Holy Land discovers how deeply embedded in the culture he is. On Amos Trust's pilgrimage visits we would stop in Beit Sahour and have a meeting with 'the three Georges', who would tell us what life was like in this town next to Bethlehem. People did not realize that they would not necessarily be the same three Georges each time! This is a town where I once asked to meet George Rishmawi, only to be asked, 'Which one? There are 48 in Beit Sahour.'

So much has been tied to the name of St George,

including the myth of the dragon and the maiden. Despite this his existence is now generally accepted, but the real story that made him a saint is a little different. Elias Chacour helps to put us straight:

'I'm sorry that the Roman Catholic Church almost fired St George, but they were wrong! And I'm happy to be a Catholic without being a Roman Catholic, because for our Oriental Church, with our Orthodox or Melkite Catholics, we have three major saints (Jesus being not only the saint, but the sanctity of the saints): Mary the Mother of God, St George and the prophet Elijah. These three are the major persons after whom we call our churches, and St George is for us one who is so important in our calendar that we pray to God through St George, we name our churches after St George, we name our boys after St George – many, many of them. I think the most common names in Oriental Christianity are George and Elijah; and George is George or Jeries – it's a kind of nickname for him. These two, George and Elijah, are painted as the strong ones: Elijah with his sword – and he killed with his sword 300 priests. He might have been the best human being, but he had no idea what ecumenism and tolerance might mean. And St George is no less violently pictured, on his horse putting his sword in the mouth of the dragon. These give us the feeling of might, and I think give a false impression of might because we have been abused by might and would like sometimes to have it to practise it against others.

'St George was an officer in the Roman army, and he was originally from Lydda. He was supposed to torture 40 martyrs, 40 Christians, and he tortured them, putting them in hot water and straight away pushing them into ice water. He saw 40 of them being killed, dying, and when they died, he saw 40 crowns coming from heaven, being put on their heads – imagine that! It was for him such an impression that he said, "If these people die for their own faith, their faith must be right," and he confessed Christ and went right away to the same torture – that's why they present St George as the protector of the Church, on his horse. There is a young lady behind him, representing the Church, he is protecting the Church. The dragon is the pagan power, the Roman Empire – you find it in the Apocalypse, in Revelation. Who is able to kill the dragon?

'George's death spoke of the presence of God in his life, while his life was an illustration of the presence of the Roman Empire to oppress people. So sometimes you live a long life with an oppressive result, and sometimes you die and you start living in the hearts of the people because your body was extinguished and you started living in God. The dragon plans to destroy, to destroy everything, and what the book of Revelation is all about is that there is hope. The dragon or evil will be devastating all through human history, but God has the last word. It's one of the most beautiful books of the New Testament.'

So Susan and Elias have helped us know the real story (or variations of the real story), and how to interpret the myth. After visiting the village of Al-Khader, our next place to look will be to follow up Elias' point, and go to the book of Revelation.

# Wednesday: The God who gives life

Revelation 2.2–7

I know your works, your toil and your patient endurance. I know that you cannot tolerate evildoers ... I also know that you are enduring patiently and bearing up for the sake of my name, and that you have not grown weary. But I have this against you, that you have abandoned the love you had at first. Remember then from what you have fallen; repent, and do the works you did at first ... Let anyone who has an ear listen to what the Spirit is saying to the churches. To everyone who conquers, I will give permission to eat from the tree of life that is in the paradise of God.

Al-Khader is a village south-west of Bethlehem. Once a Christian village, it is now Muslim but there are still signs of its Christian heritage (for instance they still make the sign of the cross on their bread). There is a major check-point here, beside the village, because there is a bypass road for settlers, and sadly many locals have been killed here. We visited the checkpoint area and watched people coming and going. There was a little market by the parking area where the road had been blocked. People push their belongings on supermarket trolleys. I watched a group of seven or eight women struggling and burdened down – one seemed very old. Here they have to carry sick people in sun or rain. It is the daily humiliation of a nation given the repeated message that they are racially inferior –

that they are trash. But even in this struggling scenario, spirit and humour come through; as we stand watching people move slowly up and down the track to the checkpoint, one humorist passing us says, waving back at the track, 'This is the road to peace.'

'If you really want to see what's going on you should come to Hell Valley or the valley of fire,' says another local, talking of the dreadfully dangerous roads that people have to use to get around the roadblocks. In front of them is a beautiful bypass road – but not for them. They are a people who once had a land but who have been occupied and colonized for centuries. They are left with no dignity and no freedom. I have a copy of the local Arabic newspaper of that day, which shows an Israeli soldier with a gun pointing at a mother and a little boy; the 11- or 12-year-old boy is crying. It is a painful picture, but this is the generation of children who have seen the humiliation of their fathers and mothers by 18-year-old soldiers; the children will never forget. An awful legacy has been bequeathed while the world has been silent.

We leave the checkpoint and go to the church of St George. If it is closed, ring the bell and they will open it for you. It is beautiful inside, wonderfully kept with recent paintings on walls and ceiling. Now there is just one monk at Al-Khader.

Apparently St George lived here for a while with his mother. We are told the same story we have heard from Elias, and hear that St George is the patron saint of all Palestine; he is the protector so his image is in all homes. St George is seen as protector and healer, the one who keeps the land green and brings happiness. *Al-Khader* means 'green', and we are told by our Bethlehem guide Wisam Salsaa that the Al-Khader story originates in Egypt and was then fused with the story of St George; it is basically the same myth as George and the dragon. Just as at Lod, those who have been healed leave rings and necklaces in front of the icon of St George. Local people have been telling us that they call out 'Khader' in an emergency; it is a cry for protection. Al-Khader church is full every Sunday, and Muslims also come from all over Palestine asking for miracles; it is considered a place of cure and they make promises such as 'I will walk without shoes from Hebron . . .' Muslims will sometimes slaughter two sheep outside as a sacrificial gift.

When the Crusaders came as an occupying force Christians fought alongside Muslims against them. To locals, St George was seen as trampling down the dragon of the Crusaders. Muslims respect him so much that they always say, 'Al-Khader – peace on him.' So maybe in St George we can find a unifying figure between Christian and Muslim. As we come out of the church I see that the flag of St George flies above the church of Al-Khader just as it would above an English parish church.

## God versus empire

But we have been reminded by Susan and Elias that the dragon in the St George myth represents evil, and Elias Chacour pointed us to the importance of the book of Revelation. Here in this remarkable and strange book St John of Patmos writes about how to live under empire. It used to be believed that Revelation was written for the Church under persecution, but Wes Howard-Brook and Anthony Gwyther in their book about Revelation say, 'The emerging consensus among historians . . . finds no evidence for a widespread or systematic persecution of Christians in first-century provincial Asia. Rather, the evidence suggests that it was seduction by the Roman Empire from within a context of relative comfort . . . that more accurately describes the situation of the original audience of the book of Revelation.' They point out that members of the Church were 'increasingly attracted to the ways of empire' (*Unveiling Empire*, Orbis Books, 1999, p. xxii).

So perhaps Revelation is more relevant to those of us living in the comfortable West than we have often assumed. The book has been used almost as a horoscope to try and read the future or to predict historical events. It has been used tragically to endorse empires and domination systems, including here in the Holy Land. It has often been read as supporting a God of domination, rather than seeing that the kingdom or community of God is in conflict with this violent and dominating view. Empire may appear to be in charge, but the faithful are called to resist.

What is empire? Howard-Brook and Gwyther say, 'When a dominant culture also has the power – whether that of seduction or of military might – to impose its cultural perspective on others, it becomes . . . "empire". Empire typically claims that its own socially constructed reality is the ultimate one, thus displacing the truly ultimate reality – where God lives and reigns – from its rightful place. The genius of empire is that it is able to establish an aura around itself that says: the way the empire is, is the way things are supposed to be' (p. 121).

## Choose your patron saint

So St George, who resisted empire, reminds us to deal with it in whatever shape or form it presents itself. There are two Georges in the stories. One becomes the saint of the

Crusaders – a symbol of domination. However, the other is faithful to Christ and is seen as healer and protector. We have to choose the George who is our patron saint.

Tony Graham, in his booklet 'Expecting the Lion – Following the Lamb: a study of Revelation' (2003), says, 'The God I believe in is the life and soul of the universe, whose nature is revealed in Jesus who came "that they might have life in all its fullness" ... But there is another god. William Blake called him "Nobodaddy up aloft" who loves war and slaughtering. He is the god who is loving to one tribe or nation or sect, to "those who are like us", but enables them to kill aliens or heretics or anyone not like them, while quoting Scripture. The god of the Crusaders and of the Inquisition and of the witch-burners ... The god who embodies lasting hatred, so that the words, "The Lord will have war with Amalek from generation to generation" (Exodus 17.15) are read so that any enemy nation can be named in place of Amalek, as some Israelis name Palestinians. There is only one God who is personal and gives life and gives power to those who struggle for peace and for justice' (p. 1).

One of the key messages of Revelation is the rejection of violence. Howard-Brook and Gwyther point out that 'vengeance is mine' (Deuteronomy 32.35) is a text frequently in the background in Revelation. 'Nowhere does Revelation authorize or glorify human violence. To the contrary, its ceding to God of the exclusive authority to act with violence when required by justice marks off this behaviour as forbidden to humanity. Human violence is a sign of the "mark of the beast".' The battle of Revelation is between the dragon's empire of evil and violence and the empire of those faithful to the ways of Jesus and non-violence.

# Thursday: The reign of God versus idolatry

Revelation 12.7–12
And war broke out in heaven; Michael and his angels fought against the dragon. The dragon and his angels fought back, but they were defeated ... The great dragon was thrown down, that ancient serpent, who is called the Devil and Satan, the deceiver of the whole world ... Then I heard a loud voice in heaven, proclaiming, 'Now have come the salvation and the power and the kingdom of our God ... they have conquered him by the blood of the Lamb and by the word of their testimony, for they did not cling to life even in the face of death.'

In Revelation 12 we find the dragon of empire in action and being defeated by angels and by the followers of 'the Lamb'. The dragon is a great deceiver, and yet this is the way of illusion supported by all sorts of propaganda praising the emperor in the Roman Empire, and supported in our time by spin, manipulation and good PR. Theologian Walter Wink sees the religion of Babylon as still powerful: 'It, and not Christianity, is the real religion of America. I will suggest that this myth of redemptive violence undergirds American popular culture, civil religion, nationalism, and foreign policy, and that it lies coiled like an ancient serpent at the root of the system of domination that has characterized human existence since well before Babylon ruled supreme' (*Unmasking the Powers: The Invisible Forces that Determine Human Existence,*

Fortress Press, 1986). For those of us from Britain, we are part of that same empire. A country that makes weapons of destruction and trades in them for our benefit is certainly doing the work of the dragon and showing Babylonian tendencies.

## The arms trade is our idol

In his booklet 'A Matter of Life and Death' (Pax Christi, 2001), Chris Cole says, 'The arms trade has become our idol – we have put our trust in the arms trade and from it we seek our salvation – and, as the prophets make clear, we have therefore become its captive.' He goes on to expand this aspect of trust and shows our economic dependence: 'Britain is the second largest arms trader in the world. Britain's sales of arms around the world are about £5–6 billion per year ... time and time again we hear the refrain of just how many jobs in this country are dependent on the arms trade ... Politically too, the arms trade is very important to us ... [it] enables us ... "to punch above our weight" and helps to keep us a world power.' He also says we place our trust spiritually in the arms trade: 'Violence is not the last resort, but usually the first ... We place our security as a nation in our ability to inflict death and destruction.' Chris Cole concludes, 'Real security does not come from arms ... but from ensuring that all have adequate resources and live in justice and peace ... the arms trade Power wants to convince us that there is to be no kingdom of God.'

The call of Revelation is to leave empire behind, to walk away from Babylon, dragons and beasts, and to walk to the kingdom of God – the New Jerusalem. So now we start to catch a glimpse not only of the horror of what is, but also the hope of what can be – the vision of what 'the 'dawn' might look like. Revelation gives the picture of the Non-violent One – the Lamb who brings a new community where the ways of God are at the centre of its life. If Babylon is the illusion, the New Jerusalem is the reality.

## Friday: Called to say 'no' and 'yes'

Revelation 21.1–4
Then I saw a new heaven and a new earth; for the first heaven and the first earth had passed away ... And I saw the holy city, the new Jerusalem coming down out of heaven from God ... See, the home of God is among mortals. He will dwell with them: they will be his peoples, and God himself will be with them; he will wipe every tear from their eyes. Death will be no more ...

For St John of Patmos, the community of God is the way of life, and the way of Babylon – the way of death – is to be defeated. Howard-Brook and Gwyther say, 'Babylon exists wherever human society becomes empire, asserting its power over creation and usurping the privileges of God. Similarly, New Jerusalem is found wherever human community resists the ways of empire and places God at the centre of its shared life.' If St George is the saint of rejection of evil and the bringer of healing, he is a good example in the struggle against empire, and a curiously seditious and hopeful patron saint!

In Revelation 21.16 we discover something very special about this city of New Jerusalem. Its height, length and breadth are equal – it is a cube. For me, it is a most special verse because it is the one I heard Martin Luther King preach on when I went to hear him in St Paul's Cathedral (on his way to pick up the Nobel Peace Prize), when I was a teenager. In his sermon he pointed out that the new city that God was building would not be an unbalanced entity with caring virtues on one side and degrading vices on the other. The most noble thing about it would be its completeness, whereas the troubles of the world are due to incompleteness.

Both Babylon and New Jerusalem have great wealth, but the wealth of Jerusalem will be used for the benefit of the community whereas Babylon's use of resources is exploitative. In Revelation 22.2 it says, 'On either side of the river is the tree of life . . . the leaves of the tree are for the healing of the nations.' The new community is a healing place – a place of life. The economy will not be built on death; it is a green place – a wonderful vision of a new dawn and a place where the St George we have discovered would feel at home. But this does not all come about 'by a passive waiting on God. Rather it is won by joining forces with God and the Lamb in active resistance to empire and creative participation in New Jerusalem. Thus the followers of God and the Lamb were called to say "no" and "yes" simultaneously . . . [to] expose the reign of death in Babylon while affirming the aspiration for new life' (Howard-Brook and Gwyther, *Unveiling Empire*, p. 192).

## We need your mother love, O God

> We need your mother love, O God, to teach us to say no
> To all the ways of violence, to all the ways of war.

Forgive us for the way we have supported evil deeds
Done in the name of our nation while we've simply
   kept our peace.

We need your mother love, O God, to teach us to say
   yes
To all the ways of beauty, to all the ways that bless
To be gentle with creation and all God's creatures too
To treat the earth with kindness, to cherish and
   renew.

We need your mother love, O God, so we're
   numbered with the meek
Forgive our need to dominate over poor and weak.
And men over women and race over race
Forgive us for the fear that hides the human face.

We need your mother love, O God, to teach us how
   to live,
A love that never forces but draws because it gives.
May we reject the pride that thinks we are the best
And that we deserve much more while others can
   have less.

(Words and music Garth Hewitt
© Chain of Love Music)

## Saturday: There's no scarcity of blessing

Revelation 21.5–7
And the one who was seated on the throne said, 'See,
I am making all things new' ... 'To the thirsty I will

give water as a gift from the spring of the water of life. Those who conquer will inherit these things, and I will be their God and they will be my children.'

## Jewish voices
In each of my books I have introduced Rabbi Jeremy Milgrom, who has been an inspiration and example of someone who lives a humble and healing lifestyle. Each week I will introduce a Jewish voice. I thought this week that Rabbi Jeremy would be good, as he has always rejected the way of domination and been committed to non-violence and peace. I asked Rabbi Jeremy how he was feeling about all that was happening:

'I don't think my vision has changed in the last few years; I'm getting used to the idea that peace is not going to happen soon. It's a long, long process. I see some really hard things happening and I don't see a change in thinking.

'Jews have been raised with this attachment to the land and this belief that putting down a settlement is the most positive way of establishing the connection. But what's clear to me today is that there is a sort of triad in Judaism of the Torah, the land and the people; and they all go together – the land of Israel, the people of Israel and the Torah of Israel. And it's clear to me that these concepts have to be kept in check by some awareness of the world; very few Jews here really understand what it means to not always be pitted against the world.'

## 'I'd like to see us living together'
'I read this Palestinian book with which I agreed; it said that it would be better if not a single settlement were removed, because the future here is going to be the

41

future of one state, and the direction of removing a few settlements and giving Palestinians some tiny bantustans will actually serve the continuation of domination; it won't bring about a situation of sharing, like in South Africa. I do have to say that the State of Israel as it is right now has to change, like South Africa changed. There has to be a relinquishing of privilege and power that would have everyone living together, which would involve the same kind of massive change that happened in South Africa.'

## Rabbi Jeremy's roots

I asked Jeremy about what prompted him to come to Israel: 'I won a Bible contest, and I came to study my roots. I was excited to discover more dimensions of Jewishness. In essence, my Judaism before I came was a family secret; when I came here it was a societal secret – a whole society was my family. It took me a long time to realize there were huge numbers of people who were excluded by that societal secret.'

## There's no scarcity of the blessing

'I want to live in this land, with the people I've gotten to know, in a situation where everyone can achieve their promise and not feel that whatever advantage the other side has is to my detriment. I was recently reading essays on violence in the Bible, and one of the writers spoke about the notion of the "scarcity of the blessing"; we think it's so scarce that we grab it and keep it from someone else. There's a great image of Esau wanting to be blessed by Isaac after Jacob has taken the blessing, and the verse is, "Don't you have a blessing for me? Did you give it all to my brother?" That's what we're feeling – but I don't feel it, I feel there's sufficient blessing for everybody. It won't work as long as we're so paranoid, so suspicious of the other.

'Judaism is a rich culture, it's creative and responsive and spiritual through all these centuries, yet right now it's very un-Jewish. To my mind there is nothing less Jewish than a situation where we are using force to marginalize someone else. We are in the midst of a colonialist endeavour marginalizing the native population. And we're doing it the same way as the English and the French did it in North America, and the Spanish and Portuguese did it in Latin America, and the Dutch and the English did it in Africa and the British in Australia. That's what we're doing! I love Israelis – I don't know if you get a chance to really hang out, maybe you need Hebrew to get Israelis really comfortable. So I've done that for three and a half decades, and my kids are Israeli – but still I think it's a huge effort to have those positive aspects of Israeli culture without the built-in positioning for power and denial.'

### 'The poison has got to us'

'So many people give so much of their time to somehow speculate or fantasize about using force. We take this fantasy of using violence as the obvious way to go and for me it's an indication of where our culture is today. And not just Israeli culture – look at George Bush, "dead or alive" and everything. Western civilization is in a real rut right now – maybe it's not Western, maybe it's a lot of places where the use of force is seen as the obvious, the noble, the only way out. But I think that's sick; the poison has really gotten to us.'

## The message of St George

So has this week given us clues as to how to make the most of St George's Day (23 April)? I think it has. In our thoughts and prayers we can remember the Palestinian Church, who have lent us St George. We can pray for healing and for delivery from evil in their situation, and throughout Israel and Palestine. We can learn to see George not as a symbol of power or to support us in war but rather for healing and as a witness against the forces of empire that we face. He was martyred for standing up against empire; maybe it helps us to be empathetic to those who are forgotten and to stand for the values of the kingdom (or community) of God against the values of war and the arms trade. St George the healer and the 'green one' becomes an example towards peace. Since *Al-Khader* means 'green' in Arabic and George is seen as protector of trees and the earth, St George's Day could have a much needed ecological emphasis as well. And because George is respected by Muslim, Christian and Jew, we are reminded that there is no 'scarcity of blessing' – we do not have to be competitive in our faith.

### Prayer

O God, let the witness of a martyr who stands for the values of your community against the powerful empire of domination remind us of the journey we must take: a journey showing compassion, mercy and justice to all so that our world might be healed and brought back from the ways of violence to the ways of wholeness. May any ideas of excluding the other be removed from our minds and lives as we realize there is no scarcity of blessing – we do not have to try and own you or define you. You have already defined us by making us in your image and showing us the example of vulnerable love. Amen.

# WEEK 3: NAUGHT FOR YOUR COMFORT IN THE SHEPHERDS' FIELDS

## Sunday: The things that belong to peace

Archbishop Tutu has said, 'There will be peace on earth. I know it. The death and resurrection of Jesus Christ puts it beyond doubt. Ultimately goodness and laughter and peace and compassion and joyfulness and forgiveness will have the last word. Jesus said "And when I am lifted up from the earth I shall draw everyone to myself." As he hangs from his cross with outflung arms, thrown out to clasp all, everyone and everything in a cosmic embrace, so that all – everyone, everything – belongs.' (*Sunday Telegraph*, Easter Sunday 2001)

One Saturday night at midnight we were on the balcony of Wisam and Rasha Salsaa's family home in Beit Sahour. Wisam's brother Rami was there and his father Tawfiq Bisharah and his mother Ayda; a few other neighbours and two visitors from the USA joined us, and we received such hospitality. They fed us and I gave an informal concert. We were joined by Rasha's father and then later by the Mayor of Beit Sahour, Fuad Kokaly and his wife. It was a beautiful and moving evening but around midnight the mayor told us the Israelis had killed the Hamas leader in Hebron. Everyone looked appalled – it was thought that there had been an agreement to stop assassinations. It

46

was a reminder of the reality of life in this area not far from Hebron.

## The death of Green Mountain

I was still thinking about this the next morning as I walked in beautiful Beit Sahour. It was a lovely morning and church bells were ringing from the Latin (Catholic) church. People were crowding in, and I left them heading to church and strolled around to enjoy the beauty. But there on a neighbouring hill was a shocking sight. It is one of the great obscenities of this world: the destroyed Jabal abu Ghoneim or Green Mountain. What would St George, the green one, have said? Here in the Shepherds' Fields, the top has been taken off the mountain. Hundreds of trees have been pulled down. And for what? To build the Har Homa settlement – a place of deep shame. It is built in direct contravention of international law. It is what Israeli academic Jeff Halper calls 'the vandalization of the Holy Land'. Here on the very Shepherds' Fields this huge settlement, full of houses, hotels and shopping malls, looms menacingly above Beit Sahour to create an alternative Bethlehem for tourists that will strangle the economy of the nearby 'little town' of Bethlehem. It is a horror to behold.

And then I saw a further obscenity, the apartheid wall tearing a swathe across the Shepherds' Fields – a wall of separation cutting right across and snaking through the fields of Ruth. Here in the very place where angels sang of the possibility of peace on earth and goodwill to all, the direct opposite was happening. Evil was being allowed to flourish to contradict that wonderfully inclusive gospel message. We need St George to deal with another dragon of evil.

I turned away. It was painful. I looked across the town – bells were now ringing from the Greek Orthodox church. Meanwhile, Apache attack helicopters came flying overhead, one hovering low for a while. I had a view of the cross of the Latin church with the helicopters as a backdrop, their noise competing with the bell ringing from the Orthodox church. This was a clear-cut Sunday morning sermon – the dragon of domination, empire, bloodshed, violence, separation and destruction of the environment versus a message of peace, community, gospel, people living in harmony and caring for the land and environment.

## An insult to God

As I walked I began to think of Archbishop Trevor Huddleston, and the way he called the Church and the world to wake up to what was happening in apartheid South Africa in the 1950s. His clarion call was the book *Naught for Your Comfort* (Collins, 1956); the title was taken from G. K. Chesterton's 'Ballad of the White Horse':

> I tell you naught for your comfort,
> yea, naught for your desire,
> save that the sky grows darker yet
> and the sea rises higher.

Trevor Huddleston said, 'What I shall try to avoid is that most common and persistent error in all such assessments – the attempt to be impartial. By this I mean that I shall write this book as a partisan, for I believe that Christians are committed in the field of human relationships to a partisan approach. I believe that, because God became Man, therefore human nature in itself has a dignity and

value which is infinite. I believe that this conception necessarily carries with it the idea that the State exists for the
individual, not the individual for the State. Any doctrine
based on racial or colour prejudice and enforced by the
State is therefore an affront to human dignity and *ipso
facto* an insult to God Himself. It is for this reason I feel
bound to oppose . . .' He goes on to challenge the policy of
the South African government at that time.

Trevor Huddleston saw it with great clarity –
attempting to be impartial in these sorts of situations
where one group of humanity is condemned simply by
virtue of the fact that they are the wrong race is not
acceptable. A friend of mine asked her bishop to speak up
about the suffering of the Palestinian Church and community. He refused, on the grounds he would be seen as anti-
Semitic. What moral cowardice and muddled thinking!
Many Jewish groups are opposing their government's
treatment of Palestinians – to suggest we should keep quiet
for fear of being thought anti-Semitic raises an interesting
question: are we? We could be, and it is always important
to look at our own motives and prejudices, but at the same
time it is patronizing to suggest that there can be no criti-
cism of the current Israeli government. It betrays the many
Israeli peace activists, both Jewish and Palestinian. (It is
important to remember that 20 per cent of Israeli citizens
are Palestinian Arabs.) But a further point raises its head:
Palestinians are a Semitic people too – are we treating
them with as much respect as we would treat Jewish
Semitic people? It is important to face anti-Jewish senti-
ments within Christian history, within the New Testament,
and in today's world. Having done that there is still an
issue to address that has not been properly dealt with for
over 50 years and is getting worse all the time; and over

the issue of the Palestinians (whether the Palestinians of the West Bank or Gaza or the Palestinians within Israel or indeed the millions of Palestinian refugees), I would have to quote Trevor Huddleston and say there is 'naught for your comfort'.

Towards the end of the book he says, 'The immediate future must be dark: darker, I believe, than it is at this moment of writing. There is no sign whatever that there is a weakening in the application of the apartheid policy: just the reverse. There is a kind of buoyant confidence in Government circles, that, in spite of world opinion, in spite of "liberalists", clerics, Communists and agitators, the African people are accepting and will continue to accept the medicine handed out to them in larger and larger and more frequent doses. I would say that, superficially, there is some justification for this buoyancy. Opposition, both on the "liberal" European front and the non-European, is presently at a low ebb, the lowest that ever I remember. "The seduction of power" is having its effect. But that this effect is temporary, I am absolutely convinced.'

He ends his book by saying, 'It is for the church to proclaim fearlessly, in season and out of season, the truth of the Gospel: and to recognise that that truth is revolutionary ... the way of apartheid is a denial of the very foundation of the Gospel itself. It is a return to the question, "Am I my brother's keeper?"; a forsaking of the question, "And who is my neighbour?" It is a denial of charity, and therefore a denial of God Himself. Nothing will persuade me otherwise ... And I KNOW the solution ... It lies in the simple recognition that ALL men ... are made in "the image and likeness of God": that in consequence each PERSON is in infinite and eternal value: that the State exists to protect the person, but is in itself always of inferior value to the person . . . Only we who, in our ordinary daily life, accept and at least try to act upon these truths, know how easy is the answer. "If thou hadst known, even thou at least in this thy day the things which belong unto thy peace. But now they are hid from thine eyes." "The things which belong unto thy peace . . ." But South Africa, like Jerusalem, is blind,' he ends. Well maybe now we could turn it round and pray that Jerusalem, like South Africa, will at last see the things that belong for peace.

## Monday: From a refugee camp to a concentration camp

✠

Psalm 140.12
I know that the LORD maintains the cause of the needy, and executes justice for the poor.

I continued with my walk and then returned to Wisam's house to meet up with those returning from church. Wisam is an official guide trained at Bethlehem University; we had intended that he would guide us not only in the West Bank but also in Israel, but he could not get permission to join us. Wisam now drove us around to see how life had changed since we were last here.

He showed us the areas of land that have been confiscated in Beit Sahour, and he said that Beit Sahour and indeed the whole West Bank is being turned from a refugee camp into a concentration camp. People are being warned that they will have to evacuate their homes because of the building of the wall; much of the land of Beit Sahour is being taken. We looked at a confiscated beautiful old house caught in the security zone around the wall. In its fields, where no one could now go, almonds, grapes, nuts and olives are growing. The Greek Orthodox Church has built a housing project in Beit Sahour on the edge of the Shepherds' Fields. It is built and supported by the Church; but now these new buildings, with families already living in them, await demolition and removal by the Israeli army. This is ironic, for right behind them is the huge ecological disaster of the new town settlement of Har Homa.

## The destruction of the hills of God

It is so peaceful and quiet as we stand on the hills of Bethlehem and Beit Sahour, but deeply shocking to see the confiscated land, the brutal social engineering with the creation of new borders, the racism that says you can build and grab land if you are Israeli but your home will be demolished if you are Palestinian. It makes visible the appalling rape of Palestine. Looking at the wall here, Wisam commented, 'It must collapse like the Berlin Wall – there's electronic wire, automatic firing, camera observation and attack dogs.' There is certainly 'naught for your comfort' here. The words of Jamal in Ibrahim Fawal's novel *On the Hills of God* come back to me: 'When I was young before I lost my eyesight . . . I wanted to write a symphony of these hills – the hills of God. I wanted to write about their glory and everlasting meaning. I wanted to write about the people who lived and still live on them.' I want to write about the people too, but most of all I want to encourage people to come and hear their story first hand.

## Resistance is not terrorism

As we stand there, in the distance we can see a Caterpillar bulldozer working away making complete apartheid a reality. From the neighbouring houses people want to give us coffee – despite everything, their hospitality remains.

We moved on to Dheishe refugee camp which has been here since 1948. There are 11,000 people in this camp, with one church and three big mosques. The Israeli army came in, in March 2002, and imposed curfews and killed many, shelling from helicopters, but international peace activists also came to live with the families to try and deter the army from its destruction. We looked at slogans on walls against the occupation and remembering the martyrs; one says, 'Resistance is not terrorism.' We chatted to some young lads – one was wearing a T-shirt showing a boy who was killed at 14, Kefah Khalei Ibbeid. Vibrant young lads as one would expect anywhere, but what is the future for them? There is 'naught for your comfort' here.

## Tuesday: A cry to the Church – 'Come and meet us in our despair'

Hebrews 13.1–5
Let mutual love continue. Do not neglect to show hospitality to strangers . . . remember those who are in prison, as though you were in prison with them; those who are being tortured, as though you your- selves were being tortured . . . Keep yourselves free from the love of money, and be content with what you have . . .

One of my good friends in Bethlehem is Bishara Awad, who is the Principal of Bethlehem Bible College. He is a very gentle and compassionate person, and I was keen to hear his views at this time. He is an Evangelical, and now is the time for the Evangelical Church to listen to him and give him their support.

'This is the worst that we have ever been witnessing and going through; the closure is very strict. People are not allowed to go to Jerusalem and people from Jerusalem are not allowed to come here. For example, yesterday we had a graduation; the Chairman of the Board is Bishop Naim Nassar, and he wanted to come from Jerusalem to be at the graduation and give a speech. They did not let him in, and he is a bishop, and this is very unusual that they will not allow a clergyman to enter Bethlehem. Once they build that wall to separate the two communities completely, then the Palestinians will certainly be in a ghetto; I'm afraid Bethlehem may become a ghetto.'

### 'My only hope is in righteous Israelis'

'There are people in the peace camp that are supportive of the Palestinian cause and want to see good things happening to the two communities, and are against the wall that's being built between the two sides – and many Israelis are against it because they say very clearly that this is not a way for peace, not a way for co-existence. We had an incident here when one of our students – a graduate student – had a piece of land just a little south of Bethlehem, and settlers wanted to take this land. Many Jews came to be there in solidarity with his family. The case is in court now and we don't know what will happen, but at least there are Israelis who are for peace, who are for justice, and I am glad of that. To me, this is my only hope. America is no hope for us, Europe is not a hopeful situation for us, and the Israeli government certainly is not. The Palestinians can't force peace, so our only hope is the Israelis themselves. I would call them righteous Israelis who can see their future ahead of them and actually want to see peace.'

### 'All my dreams have been shattered'

'In the last thirty years I never thought I would ever come to the point of despair, but in the last two years, yes, I am beginning to feel that way. I am a man of faith and as such I should never really despair, so I will always be hopeful. But to me, all my dreams have been shattered, my dreams of being here. I could be in America, and have become an American citizen. I have always encouraged my children that they should be here and they should build this Palestinian nation together. I have two children in America, and I don't have the guts to tell them, now you've finished college, come and live here. There is nothing for them, absolutely nothing for them. Sami is here but I want the whole family to be here together. So really my dreams that have been nurtured since I was a student in America are shattered.'

### 'Jesus left heaven to be with us here – so you church people come too'

'I'm thankful for those who are supportive in the Church, who are praying for us, who stand by us – and there are thousands of those. But there are also millions of others who don't even know that we exist, and many times they are surprised to find out there are Palestinian Christians. So I would like to tell the Church outside, please look us up, find out about us, study the situation and study about the Church. The Church of Jesus Christ started right here.

These are the roots and there is still a living Church here. So come and learn about us. Jesus left heaven incarnated to the earth to be with us, so you church people come and be with us.

'I feel we are in an apartheid situation. In Israel and here in the West Bank, there are roads that are only for the Jews, for the settlers; no Palestinians are allowed to be on them. There are laws that are put especially for the Israelis, other laws for the Palestinians, so there is discrimination very clearly. Unfortunately many churches, especially the right-wing churches, are just supportive of Israel whether it is right or wrong and they are not willing to look at issues at all. So I feel sad that church people are like that.'

## Wednesday: The gift of non-violence

Luke 1.78–79
By the tender mercy of our God, the dawn from on high will break upon us, to give light to those who sit in darkness and in the shadow of death, to guide our feet into the way of peace.

*Memories of Christmas 2002*
Sami Awad is Bishara's son and works for the Holy Land Trust. Christmas 2002 was a very difficult time for him and his wife Rana. This is part of the email he sent round at that time:

To our friends,

With hearts full of sadness I write this letter a couple of days before Christmas to inform you that Israeli army troops have occupied the apartment building we live in and have locked us as well as twelve other families in our apartments. They have told us that they are here for an indefinite period of time and we will not be able to leave our apartments until they leave.

This afternoon (23 December 2002, 5.00 p.m.), as volunteers (Bob and Margaret) and myself were going around Bethlehem passing out gifts donated to needy families through the Holy Land Trust, we got a call from a neighbour who said that the Israeli army had stormed our building and had forced all residents out of their homes and into one apartment. We immediately tried to return in order to see what was happening and to at least be present if the army decided to enter our apartment. When we got close, we were welcomed by Israeli soldiers pointing their machine-guns at us and yelling at us to go back. An hour later I tried again ... we were escorted to our apartment, we were told to leave the door key in the outside keyhole. When I asked why, one soldier turned his head and walked away in what I think was a sign of shame; the other said, 'To lock you in.' Yes – lock us in our home!

Christmas is two days away and we are prisoners in our home. This is our gift this holiday season. This year was going to be our baby girl's first Christmas ... Even with the siege of Bethlehem and the continued curfews and suffering, we still decorated the tree, bought the gifts, took out the Christmas CDs and thought that at the least we will be able to celebrate Christmas with our families. It seems that even this simple wish will not come true this season and we will be celebrating Christmas as prisoners locked in our home . . .

Please pray for our safety. We do not even know what the next hour will bring us. We hear the soldiers walking up and down the staircase and we also heard them destroy furniture in the apartment below us. Are we next? We do not know!

I can only conclude this letter by saying that from the bottom of our hearts and from this holy place, we wish you a Merry Christmas.

In peace,
Sami Awad

As the news of what was happening in the Bethlehem area came in, email after email, around Christmas 2002 I wrote this song:

*They've cancelled Christmas in Bethlehem*

They've cancelled Christmas in Bethlehem
They've cancelled Christmas in Bethlehem
In a land once known as Holy the gun is in control
They've cancelled Christmas in Bethlehem

They've cancelled freedom in Bethlehem
They've cancelled freedom in Bethlehem
An occupation army has invaded Palestine
They've cancelled Christmas in Bethlehem

Though angels are singing, F-16s drown out the sound
Though angels are singing, the tanks are much too
loud
And those who sing of peace on earth will this year
sing in vain
Because the Israeli army have closed down Bethlehem

They've cancelled wise men in Bethlehem
They've cancelled shepherds in Bethlehem
They've stopped the wise men at the checkpoint and
the shepherds can't leave home
They're under curfew in Bethlehem

Though angels are singing . . .

They've cancelled hope in Bethlehem
They've cancelled peace in Bethlehem
O Holy Child, what would you say – you're unwel-
come once again
They've cancelled Christmas in Bethlehem

(Words and music Garth Hewitt
© Chain of Love Music)

## *The Holy Land Trust*

The Holy Land Trust is based in Bethlehem and tries to strengthen and improve the lives of children, families and communities in Palestine through a wide variety of programmes. On this visit we dropped into their offices; Sami was away but George S. Rishmawi was there and he gave us an update on their work:

'In the Holy Land Trust we have three departments; first, Remember the Innocents. Remember the Innocents is so called because Herod is still alive, and the Palestinian children of Bethlehem are still persecuted and killed; for instance the woman and her son who were killed near the Church of the Nativity during the first day of the invasion last year (April 2002). So now we have an active Remember the Innocents club, and they are preparing a big party for children that we are holding in Bethlehem. In addition to this we have a Remember the Innocents festival, an annual festival in Manger Square on 28 December. We publish our own music, really good music for children, sung by children, very nice music in Arabic. We've just finished four festivals in four different cities – Jericho, Hebron, Bethlehem and Ramallah.

'The next department is Travel and Encounter; yesterday I was working with a delegation from faculties of various universities in the US. We have a delegation from our office in LA. We have the headquarters here, and then the LA support office, and they started organizing delegations for us, which is very good. Then in addition we have a lot of other delegations; we have a football team from York coming in September! In Travel and Encounter now we're trying to do research as well as visits. We're going to research 10 to 20 villages, because the roots of the Palestinians can be found in the villages, where the lifestyle has not changed much in thousands of years.

'In addition to this, we have the Peace and Reconciliation department – we have just finished a three-month group training in non-violence for Bethlehemites. They have been trained and now they will be trainers; phase two of the project is to write a manual for non-violence training; it will be finished in two weeks. It is going to be the first manual in the Arab world for non-violence training in Arabic, and we are sending it to Iraq. We start immediately training the Jenin community, the

Jenin university and the Jenin refugee camp, from 6 to 12 July (2003).'

I asked George if he would encourage people to come to the Holy Land. 'I would say, come with an open mind and an open heart, because reality is shocking. Come and witness what's going on. I believe the itinerary of a delegation is an art. We do all kinds of delegations, inter-faith, Christian–Christian, Muslim–Muslim, cultural tourism, even sightseeing.'

## Thursday: Jerusalem – in the heart and in olive wood

Psalm 88.4–9
I am like those who have no help, like those forsaken among the dead . . . like those you remember no more . . . I am shut in so that I cannot escape . . . Every day I call on you, O LORD.

### At home with the Salsaa family
Tawfiq Bisharah Salsaa has been working in olive wood since 1952. His work in crafts had started even earlier, when at ten years old he started to work in mother-of-pearl, making brooches, crosses, jewellery boxes, frames for pictures and covers for the Koran. After the 1967 war there were no orders or interest in those things, so Tawfiq learnt carving in olive wood. The 1970s were the best time for olive wood sales, as tourists began to return after the 1967 war. Each week he would carry boxes to Jerusalem, and his boxes were so popular that merchants would fight

to buy. Then in 1973 tourism stopped again due to the Yom Kippur war, but after this it picked up again until the first Intifada. Beit Sahour was under curfew in the first Intifada; after Oslo the situation improved but the second Intifada has stopped everything.

As a response to this total drying up of work Tawfiq embarked on the work of a lifetime – he has made a model of the Old City of Jerusalem in olive wood. It has taken three years; he has done it from memory, and it is an absolutely remarkable piece of work. I asked him why he had done it:

'I thought this would be a long Intifada so I wanted to make something new – carving is enjoyable and whenever I am not working I don't feel good. Jerusalem is close to my heart so I thought I would make Jerusalem here. I did it from memory.'

It has taken over their front room, and Tawfiq would prefer it to be in a museum so many people can see it. For 32 years he used to go to Jerusalem twice a week and walk it widely each time, so he knows it by heart. 'No one in all this region has ever spent three years doing one piece of work like this.' In 1915, at the age of about 30, Tawfiq's father did the carvings on the front of the altar at the Latin church in Beit Sahour. They are remarkable, and it is well worth stopping to take a look at them. His father was obviously extremely talented but Tawfiq says, 'artists were not appreciated in those days'.

It is hard to even start to describe Tawfiq's model of Jerusalem; its detail is staggering. Tawfiq will need to sell it to survive; he knows he could sell it out of the country but he would really like it to remain in the Bethlehem area. I thought how wonderful it would be if it could be put on display in the Peace Centre in Manger Square; this beautiful new building, which was finished in time for the Millennium, was horribly trashed and soiled by the Israeli army when they occupied it in April 2002. It would be good now to have an example on display of someone using their hands in such a creative way during that shameful time.

## Palestinian tour guides

Wisam Salsaa is one of Tawfiq's sons. When I first met him he was the youngest Palestinian guide; I was looking forward to working and travelling with him to get material for this book, but he could not travel out of the Bethlehem area. Instead, he organized two other guides, Khalil Harouny in Galilee and Rimon Maklouf, the lecturer who had trained him at Bethlehem University, to go with me in Jerusalem. All three are Christian guides and their knowledge and insight is quite remarkable, whether it's history, holy sites or theology. These Christian guides are struggling to survive; they are not being used at all at present. I believe it is important for Christian pilgrims to return now, but only if they do tours which meet the 'living stones'. To do these sorts of tours properly it is invaluable to have a Christian tour guide from Bethlehem, Nazareth or Jerusalem. Amos Trust has been building links with the 'living stones' for many years and has been taking pilgrimages regularly; we stopped for two years because of all the problems, and concentrated on bringing peacemakers from both the Palestinian and Israeli communities to the UK to update and inform people of what was happening on the ground. We now think it is time to take groups back as soon as possible to hear first hand and to experience the kind of pilgrimage reflected in this book. So Amos Trust plans to take again each year starting in 2004. Part of our reason is to support the Christian guides and the churches of the 'living stones', to support the economy of those who make a living from pilgrimages, and to encourage Jewish and Muslim peacemakers.

## 'Life here is worth nothing'

On my last day in Bethlehem, after our tour seeing the wall and the checkpoints and talking to people, I sat with Wisam and talked about how he was feeling.

'The only thing that we have right now is hope and faith, otherwise we're going to leave, because if you think about life here, it's worth nothing, and you have nothing to do. It's meaningless. I wake up in the morning and I don't know what I have to do. I don't have a job, I don't have anything, I am not able to make any plans for the future, not even for the near future. Some people think that we get used to living in these conditions, but we never do; we are always angry and mad inside and carry an anger against the occupation, or against those who are practising this pressure against us. For many people, especially young people, they have a dream now, and this dream is to emigrate, to leave Palestine. And today, the promised land for Palestinians is the United States – or, let's say, the promised land is mainly Michigan and California, many families go there.

'We don't have the basic rights for humans; for example, I cannot travel, I cannot leave Bethlehem, I have not left Bethlehem for six months. There is really nothing to do. I have tried to be active in my community, but it's not easy to be active. Closure means that we are living in a big jail, or even a small jail where you cannot get out of your town, you cannot get to your school, you cannot get to hospitals. So closure is lock-down, you can do nothing.'

*Worth less than a donkey*

'I'll tell you a story: once there was a demonstration here in Bethlehem. Children were throwing rocks at Israeli soldiers standing at Rachel's Tomb, and the children saw a donkey, a white donkey, so they painted David's star on the donkey, and they pushed the donkey towards the soldiers. That made the soldiers mad, and they started to shoot at the children. One of the journalists asked a soldier, "Why didn't you kill the donkey?" He said, "Because of the animal rights organizations, they would be mad at us" So I think the way they treat us is less than a donkey – they treat animals better than they treat us.'

# Friday: The dividing wall

Ephesians 2.14
For he is our peace; in his flesh he has made both groups into one and has broken down the dividing wall, that is the hostility between us.

Israeli activist Dr Jeff Halper is Professor of Anthropology at Ben Gurion University. He is co-ordinator of the Israeli Committee against House Demolitions (www.icahd.org). He is a committed peace activist, and having seen the awful scar of the wall and seen the terrible impact it is making I asked him his view.

*Separation from the Palestinians*
'The wall is called by Israel "the separation fence"; in fact it's a wall. It's about 50 metres wide and much thicker

than the Berlin Wall. So it's tremendously invasive and a massive military fortification. It's also not on the border, but it goes from 2 to up to 20 miles or more inside Palestinian areas, so there'll be something like 100,000 Palestinians trapped permanently between the wall and the border. Also thousands of olive trees have been uprooted. One of the terrible things is that it has become very fashionable for people in the richer suburbs of Tel Aviv, and shopping centres, to buy old olive trees that are uprooted from these places. Agricultural land is destroyed; there are wells that people have no access to any more; so the impact economically, demographically, in terms of freedom of movement is terrible, creating prisons for people, ghettos.'

## Separation from the Middle East

'I think there's a deeper level as well, and in a way it's not only separation from the Palestinians, but I think you can see the wall as a separation from the Middle East in general. Last April, 2002, when the Saudis with the backing of the Arab League offered Israel regional integration – not just peace and recognition, but actual integration into the region – if it would give up its occupation, Israel said, "No." I think Israel has no interest in being part of the Middle East; it faces Europe, it has its back to the Middle East and now its back to the wall, and in a sense I think Israel sees itself as a Singapore, that's the image that's used all the time when Israel is thinking of its economic future. It's disconnected from the surrounding regions that it's a part of, and it's oriented economically, culturally, socially, politically, toward Europe and the States.'

## An attacking wall

'Of course, what lets Israelis off the hook is the idea that "Well, we offered the Palestinians 95 per cent at Camp David, and they refused in violence, and so they deserve anything they get, they brought this on themselves, so we're not responsible, we don't have to feel bad about it." So you can construct a whole rationale to justify it completely – it frees you of any responsibility or guilt. The Palestinians forced us to build the wall. Golda Meir once said she was very angry that the Arabs forced us to kill their kids in wars – that twisted kind of logic. For the Palestinians, of course, it's terrible, and I think that's also part of the equation: that if it gets bad enough they'll leave. So you might look at a kind of a transfer element to the wall. And the wall is a very dynamic thing; it's dynamic economically, in taking land, in moving Palestinians eastward, away from the border, in securing areas for Israel. It's also an attacking wall, it's very aggressive, it has dogs, killer dogs, attached to it, like the Berlin Wall did – there's a whole breed of dogs from Holland that has been brought in. It has mobile military patrols, it has self-shooting automatic guns, it's got sensory things. It's very intrusive, and it's very aggressive – it's not the kind of wall that makes good neighbours.'

## Jewish voices

I asked Jeff about his view of Israel and what brought him to Israel: 'I returned because my Jewish identity is very important, and I built into that these other values, and I probably idealized Judaism to a certain degree. That's how I related to the world, and so for me it was a natural progression; I became Israeli in a national sense before I even went to Israel, because I was more than just an ethnic

Jew. The ethnic Judaism didn't satisfy me, so Judaism became a primary identity, but it wasn't religious, so it was natural that it would be a national identity.

'I depart from many Palestinians and Arabs, and some of the most critical Israelis, who simply dismiss Israel as a European settler colonial state, because I think there really was a general claim to the land. It was that the Jews really felt, both for purposes of national identity and also because of persecution, that it was important for them to come back to the land, that they were coming back in a genuine return. It didn't represent most Jews, but there was a genuine idea that this is our homeland; we have a claim.

'But I think (and of course, you're always reading back in hindsight) that had they come with that attitude of saying to the Arabs living there, "Look, this is our homeland, we really have a tie to it, we want to come back, it's a refuge as well, but we acknowledge and recognize that you are here, and let's see if we can work something out," I think there wasn't an inevitable conflict between the Jews and the Arabs. In fact, there are many cases in which they got along well, so that could have been worked out, but you know that's hindsight.'

## Saturday: The siege at the Church of the Nativity

Isaiah 3.14–15
. . . What do you mean by crushing my people, by grinding the face of the poor?

Whenever I am in Bethlehem, I like to visit the Church of the Nativity; it is my favourite church in the Holy Land. As I went there this time with Wisam I asked him about the siege at the church in 2002.

## The safest place was where Jesus was born

Wisam said, 'People were bleeding and starving and the bell-ringer was killed. They had a balloon over the church with a camera, and an electronic machine-gun to target any movement. Every day we heard shelling and bombs – this area was a closed military zone. A friend of mine was bleeding to death outside – he died bleeding and no one helped him – he was shot in the leg. They used machines to disturb mobiles, to scramble them, so connection was lost with the church. They had big loudspeakers and made disturbing sounds. There was a terrible noise for the surrounding areas, and it was causing deep stress on people in the church. The safest place was where Jesus was born – it was away from shots.' Wisam then said it would be good to meet someone who was in the siege, and we went to meet Jerias Kanewati.

Jerias, whose family own a souvenir shop just next to the church, was in the siege, and he told me about his experience:

'It was 1 April 2002. One or two soldiers came into town first, and then suddenly from every direction there were thousands of soldiers, with tanks and helicopters. Everyone was afraid, there was shooting from the helicopters, and bombs, and most people ran away. I tried to go home, but soldiers were in our house. So I slept outside for two days, then I called a friend and he said, "We're in the church." I managed to get inside and expected 50 to 75 inside, but found 248. I came in the back door and found the church full between the columns. I wanted to leave but they said I'd be shot. They were shooting from the balloon with the electronic gun and telescope. The first week was OK, but the Fathers said there was no food after the first week, so people were going out to get food. One young man was shot. Nearby houses were lowering food to the church, but one night a bag was dropped and so soldiers stopped it. After three weeks, the International Solidarity Movement volunteers came in and brought food and drink, but in the last few days people were very ill. There was no water.

'One person was killed in front of St George's Greek Orthodox chapel, and one in front of the Christmas bells. Eight were killed, all inside the compound, and one who escaped was shot in Manger Square. The machine-guns were so accurate and they used dum-dum (expanding) bullets. One was shot in Casanova Guest House looking for food; he said, "I love you, I don't want to leave you, I want to see my family again," but he bled to death. Part of an adjoining building was set on fire by the soldiers when they tried to get in. Two upper rooms at the side were burnt. They had two bodies inside the church, but soldiers wouldn't let them take them out – for 14 days they were inside.'

## 'This place has protected me'

'People inside respected the place; I am a Christian, and Muslims and Christians respected it. The wounded were put in the grotto where Jesus was born. Initially ten injured were brought into the church and 25 more were injured during the siege. Most people attended Mass at Easter; some Muslims made the sign of the cross. I asked one why; he said, "Because this place has protected me."

They apologized to the Fathers, who said, "Today the building is not important; we care about your lives and want you to go back to your families." Negotiations were going on in two places, Bethlehem and Ramallah, through Hannan Asser (the mayor) and the Palestinian Legislative Council. The IDF kept increasing the numbers of wanted ones – they said, "We want a list of who is inside with their ID numbers, and we will decide who's wanted." Arafat said, "Only if those inside decide to sign – I will not give ID numbers to the IDF." So those inside did sign – 26 were sent to Gaza, 13 to Europe and the rest were put in a military place called Etzion. One week after the siege, they arrested all they could find who had been inside the church. During the siege soldiers tried to invade many times and blew in the side door. Two or three times they tried from the garden. Inside there were 75 fighters, 60 police with uniforms, and the rest were civilians who had been watching a movie and ran to the church. The fighters wanted to shoot, but the order came from the leader of intelligence and Arafat saying, "Don't shoot from the church," and they said they would follow that order, though they saw the soldiers and could have shot them.'

## The International Solidarity Movement

Ghassan Andoni of the Rapprochement Centre in Beit Sahour is a remarkable man. He, along with others, has built up the International Solidarity Movement, which has become well known through films such as *Jeremy Hardy vs the Israeli Army*. Their sudden entrance into the Church of the Nativity during the siege bringing food received much publicity. But the tragic killings and woundings by the Israeli army have particularly drawn the world's attention. Names such as Rachel Corrie, who lost

71

her life when a bulldozer ran over her despite the fact she was clearly visible, as she was trying to stop the demolition of the house of a Palestinian doctor in Gaza. Tom Hurndall was shot as he tried to get children out of the way of danger, and Brian Avery had half of his face shot away. However, this movement has been very important in letting the world know about the nature of the occupation and the daily danger Palestinians are facing.

I asked Ghassan Andoni about the Rapprochement Centre and the work of ISM: 'Our only project in the last two and a half years has been founding and continuing the International Solidarity Movement, and trying to provide the support needed for the work of the Palestinian and international volunteers. Now we have another project, on media; we are trying to combine Palestinian media people and international media people to try to establish a Palestinian media service, which Western media might consider as a reliable source of information.

'There have been times when we felt we were doing something about the occupation. There were sad times, and there were good times, but we are pretty proud of what was established with the International Solidarity Movement. Our motivation is that we felt very deeply that we needed to engage in the struggle, we cannot just stand and watch it . . . You have to get your hands dirty.'

## The need to wage peace
'We need to wage peace. You have to have the guts and the courage to stand for it. If you don't, then warriors win, because they have the guts and the courage, they have the gun, they are trained and ready to die for it. We are happy that we managed to create an international movement, a real international movement that covers all the continents

and has had people from about 40 different countries. We are very happy that many people who join us are Jewish. It's a very disciplined movement; and we insist we have the right to stand against the Israeli army when they are doing collective punishment against innocent civilians.'

I asked Ghassan if he is hopeful of peace coming. He said, 'Who can tell? This is the Holy Land! There are lots of surprises. It was very unlikely in South Africa when the change happened, so never lose hope. Keep working and never lose hope. I have faith in my people – it's the only faith I have. The most terrible thing that can happen to Palestinians is to be ignored. I think most Palestinians think that when that happens, Israel wins.'

## Prayer

O God, they brought the wounded to your birthplace, the birthplace of the Prince of Peace. May those of us who are his followers have the courage to wage peace, by listening to those who are ignored, by being aware, refusing to be silent, and by showing your love equally to all people so your reign becomes a reality on earth as it is in heaven. Amen.

# WEEK 4: TOWARDS LIBERATION AND ASCENSION

## Sunday: 300,000 volunteers

Isaiah 65.21–23a
They shall build houses and inhabit them; they shall plant vineyards and eat their fruit.
They shall not build and another inhabit; they shall not plant and another eat . . . They shall not labour in vain.

*A Sunday prayer*

Lord Jesus, set my heart on doing good –
merrily and eagerly,
tenderly and carefully,
madly and passionately –
with all the gladness that flooded the great, green
    earth
with heart and healing
on that Sunday when life came leaping from the
    tomb. Amen.

(Peter Graystone/Christian Aid)

This is the week of the Ascension, so later in the week we will head back to Jerusalem to visit the Church of the Ascension and other sites there. In the church calendar in Britain and Ireland, normally in the week before

Ascension Day comes Christian Aid Week. This week has an extraordinary effect as 300,000 volunteers go knocking on doors to let the community know that we have not forgotten the poorest of the world. Volunteers stream out from 20,000 churches to do what is often an awkward task, but it lets our community know that the Church has not forgotten the poor, nor have we, nor has God. It is a remarkable witness, an ecumenical venture that is not just a very successful fundraising event: many churches also take the opportunity to make the issues of justice and compassion for the poor a key component in their services, praying for the work and for Christian Aid partners and learning more about them.

In Israel and Palestine Christian Aid have many partners, both Israelis and Palestinians. In 2003 Christian Aid launched a report called *Losing Ground: Israel, Poverty and the Palestinians* (Christian Aid, 2003). Its conclusions opened many people's eyes to what is actually happening on the ground. It pointed out the 'dramatic plunge by ordinary Palestinians into extreme poverty': 'The foundations for impoverishment were laid long ago ... Palestinians have seen the promise of a secure future stripped away – by the progressive loss of land from 1948 onwards and by successive military incursions marked by violence, land occupation and the subordination of the Palestinian economy to the Israeli economy.'

The report says that the responsibility for the current humanitarian crisis rests 'principally with Israel's military occupation of the Palestinian Territories', and that the key structures creating poverty are loss of land, settlements, Israeli control over access to water, closure and curfew, and lack of strong self-government. Christian Aid played an important part in standing against the apartheid regime of South Africa, and bringing the churches on board in that struggle. It is significant that they too recognize once again that there is 'naught for your comfort'.

Their report was written before the 'security wall' was so advanced. The Bishop of Exeter, Michael Langrish, has since visited the wall with Christian Aid and said, 'The Berlin Wall is nothing to this.' The Bishop of Brechin, Neville Chamberlain, was also on the trip and he said, 'I am deeply, deeply shocked that a world that fought and argued for the demolition of a wall around a city is now standing by as the greater wall is being built around a whole people.' The bishops saw the imprisoning of Qalqilya and Bishop Neville said, 'We saw farmers driving out to the fields who were just not able to get back again.'

Today's passage from Isaiah is a beautiful picture of a just world where agricultural land is not stolen, homes are not destroyed, farmers are not cut off from their fields, labour is not in vain. Together we must commit ourselves to pray, campaign and work to make this vision become a reality.

## Monday: The Qalqilya ghetto

Psalm 140.12
I know that the LORD maintains the cause of the needy, and executes justice for the poor.

While I was on this visit to Israel/Palestine my daughter Abi (who works for Oona King MP) was also there. They both, together with Dr Jenny Tonge MP, had been brought out by Christian Aid to see the current situation. Their trip was full of incidents, particularly as they entered Gaza at a very sensitive time. However, the phone call from Abi that sticks most in my mind was the one she made as she was looking at the wall at Qalqilya. She was clearly deeply shocked and said, 'I never thought in my lifetime I would see something like this – I feel I have walked on to a film set – or something not of this age.' Later she commented, 'I couldn't comprehend that the wall would continue for 360 kilometres. It seemed so hideous and not real. Shops and houses have been destroyed and agricultural land taken to make room for the wall. The school playground has the wall right next to it – it is what the children see from the playground all the time.'

When Abi, the Christian Aid staff and the MPs tried to get into Qalqilya a soldier, holding a grenade in his hand, said, 'Get back in the vehicle or I will throw this grenade.' A policeman dropped the driver's ID on the ground and almost ran him over as he scrabbled for it. If even British MPs get this degree of harassment, what on earth happens to the locals?

## *Jewish voices: These policies marginalize moderates and strengthen extremists*
Oona King, who is Labour MP for Bethnal Green and Bow, and is Jewish herself, said afterwards:

'The policies currently used to control the Palestinian population are: collective punishment; expropriation of land; confiscation of property; arbitrary detention; torture; routine humiliation; demeaning bureaucracy for even the smallest task; freedom of movement restricted without (or even with) appropriate permits; basic utilities such as water and healthcare withheld; a wall built to seal them off ... These policies marginalize moderates and strengthen extremists.

'I was disturbed by a visit to the town of Qalqilya on the West Bank. Qalqilya is the first community to be hermetically sealed by the security wall. The wall has encaged the city, bringing devastating effects. Almost half of the West Bank's freshwater resources come from the Western Aquifer which rests under Qalqilya, and Qalqilya will lose at least 13 groundwater wells. This is having disastrous effects on the day-to-day lives of the community. In the Jewish community, we should remember what it is like to be sealed off from the outside world. Local Israelis who used to trade with Qalqilya have had the courage to demonstrate in the streets against their own government about this wall.

'I am also convinced that most decent-minded Israelis, if they actually saw what happened in their name, would not agree with it. Like, for example, the experience of the Palestinian father whose children were blown up by an army trip wire: they were put in a taxi with their limbs, but then weren't allowed past the checkpoint to get medical help because the soldier said they didn't have the correct permit. Two of them bled to death in the back seat, the third, whom I met, has no legs and only one arm. That doesn't distinguish him from the many Israeli victims of appalling terror. What distinguishes him and his family is that although they were innocent civilian victims (aged 16, 13 and 11), they were denied access to medical treatment because of their ethnic background. We have to stop the cycle of violence ... After the experience of the Jewish people, I personally think we have a moral obligation to speak out against policies like this that have even a passing resemblance to those that caused us so much pain and agony.'

Here is a prayer by Peter Graystone from Christian Aid's Churches Team that I particularly like, as it asks for the ways of God's reign to become a reality.

## God of justice

God of all times and places, who brings light into the world's darkness, we come to you with our prayers;
so that the children may no longer be denied education;
so that the sick may no longer die from curable diseases;
so that the workers may no longer be cheated of justice;
your kingdom come:
*your will be done on earth as it is in heaven.*

So that financial systems may no more burden the poorest;
so that our trade may no more deny a fair wage;
so that debt may no more trap nations in poverty;
your kingdom come:
*your will be done on earth as it is in heaven.*

So that the innocent will walk free from prison;
so that minorities will live without fear;
so that the whole earth will worship in freedom;
your kingdom come:
*your will be done on earth as it is in heaven.*

(Peter Graystone/Christian Aid)

# Tuesday: The city of healing

Luke 6.20–49

Then he looked up at his disciples and said: '. . . Blessed are you when people hate you, and when they exclude you, revile you, and defame you on account of the Son of Man' . . . 'Do not judge, and you will not be judged; do not condemn, and you will not be condemned. Forgive, and you will be forgiven; give, and it will be given to you.'

Before heading down to Jerusalem for the Ascension we will spend a couple of days in Galilee, first of all visiting Shefa'Amr, and meeting Fuad and Ha'ana Dagher and the church where Fuad is vicar:

'My church is St Paul's Episcopal Church in Shefa'Amr. We have 200 members who make up 54 families. Four families live in Ibillin, ten minutes' drive away. We are very close to the city of Nazareth, the city where our Lord spent most of his time.

'Shefa'Amr means "healing" – we always think of our church as a means of healing on a spiritual, social and even economic basis, so the name challenges us as a church to be an instrument of healing, especially in this period of time in which we're living.

'We have very strong relationships and close links with the other denominations in Shefa'Amr; the biggest congregation is the Greek Melkite Church of St Peter and St Paul, with 8,000 members. Shefa'Amr is a Catholic city actually, a Greek Melkite Catholic city. We have the Latin (Roman)

Catholic Church of St Joseph, as well as the Greek Orthodox church, which is the smallest congregation in Shefa'Amr. Many of their members are originally from the neighbouring villages, especially Sakhnin. So we have a very strong relationship between denominations, Anglican, Roman Catholic, Greek Melkite, as well as the Greek Orthodox.

'Another thing about the city of Shefa'Amr – it is one of the unique cities within the State of Israel, since we have three religious groups, Christians, Muslims and Druze; Shefa'Amr has 35,000 people – the Christian community make up 28 per cent of the whole population, the Druze community 16 per cent, and the rest are Muslims. The good thing about Shefa'Amr is the co-existence between the three religious groups. We have many ecumenical programmes with the other religious groups; on feasts and special occasions we go and meet each other.'

### Arab Christian Israelis

Fuad then spoke of the particular problems that Israeli Arabs face.

'A problem which we face as Arab Christian Israelis living within the State of Israel is that even though I carry the Israeli passport and Israeli ID, I still constitute a third-class citizen. I am not treated equally as Jewish people are treated by the government. This shows itself in issues of daily life, such as budgets. Our municipalities, our schools, our hospitals, our institutions do not get the same budgets as Israeli institutions. Plus, our students go to the Israeli universities, such as Haifa University or even Jerusalem University, but they are not treated equally. They are always looked upon as Arabs, and they don't get the same benefits. They tell us, "You don't serve in the army as we do, so you don't get the same privileges as we get."'

## Equal rights

'Everybody speaks about getting rights, students in the university shout to get their rights and to be treated equally. Each in his or her own way is a Martin Luther King. We as a Church as well, we are like Martin Luther King in our faith and in our theology and in our outreach. If you consider me to be an Israeli citizen and you claim this is a democratic state, you have to treat us equally.'

I asked if the Arab minority pay similar taxes. 'Yes, exactly the same as any Jew who lives in the State of Israel.'

## Proud of the Church

'As a Church, I think we should work hard to find an alternative instead of killing people, on both sides. I think the alternative is to help both sides to sit together, to try to break walls which separate us from each other. The leaders from both sides need a readiness to hear what the Church has to say, and the leaders of the Church in the Middle East are not silent. I am very proud of our leaders – I speak of the Patriarch Michel Sabbah, our bishop, Bishop Riah, and other Christian leaders. I am very proud of what they say, but unfortunately no one is listening. The Christian leaders asked to meet with Sharon and other Israeli leaders; they refused. We are the voice crying in the wilderness, but no one is listening.'

# Wednesday: A hot lunchtime in Ibillin

Luke 6.27–36
But I say to you that listen, Love your enemies, do
good to those who hate you, bless those who curse
you, pray for those who abuse you. If anyone strikes
you on the cheek, offer the other also; and from
anyone who takes away your coat do not withhold
even your shirt. Give to everyone who begs from you;
and if anyone takes away your goods, do not ask for
them again. Do to others as you would have them do
to you ... love your enemies, do good ... Be merciful,
just as your Father is merciful.

Close to Shefa'Amr is Ibillin, and here Greek Melkite
priest and peace campaigner Abuna Elias Chacour has
built the remarkable Mar Elias Educational Institution,
which I have been visiting since it was a small school. It
started as a high school in September 1982, and the
struggle to get permissions for the different stages of development makes a story in itself. The school provides much
needed education for the Arab community of Western
Galilee but it has a policy of building good relationships
between Muslims, Christians, Druze and Jews – 'We work
to create an oasis where all can meet on the basis simply
of their humanity.' For some time Abuna Elias has had a
vision for a university and he has been seeking permission;
he was on my flight back, and he told me with delight that
the necessary permissions for the university had just come
through.

## Stronger than the storm

The hill on which the school stands and where the university will be is called the Mountain of Light. The whole project is a witness to light and peace. Abuna took me into the newly built auditorium downstairs from the Church of the Sermon on the Mount that is also being built. On the wall there is a mural which has a verse from Isaiah 40.22–23 over the top, along with a rainbow, 'It is he who sits above the circle of the earth who brings princes to naught.' Then on the right-hand side are the words 'Together we are stronger than the storm', a favourite saying of Elias. Underneath the rainbow are two people embracing, with the words 'Esau ran to meet him and fell on his neck and kissed him and they wept.' These are words from Genesis 33.4 where the great reconciliation occurs between Esau and Jacob. From this scene radiates a picture of people linking arms together; one of the two faces we can see is Asel Asleh, a student at the school who was killed by the Israeli Defence Force on 13 October 2000 (he was one of the 13 Israeli Arabs killed on that day). He was the leader of Seeds of Peace, an international youth peace movement whose membership cuts across all the divides. The other face in the mural is that of the peace activist Rachel Corrie of the International Solidarity Movement, who was killed by the IDF in Gaza.

## Life is a procession of funerals on both sides

I asked Abuna Elias about how he viewed the current situation in the world. He said, 'I think that our faith as Christians is a major factor for us to keep hope and to avoid sinking into hopelessness. We are shattered with the vocabulary that we hear from leaders of this world, who have only words of vengeance, of settling accounts, of killing people. I will tell you a short story of how our kids react to what is going on. One of the kids in the fifth grade at Mar Elias Institution wrote a letter that he thought he would send to the leaders of this world. And he says, "Dear Leaders, I am a little kid, I want to remind you that God has given us a small heart that he put in our body, not only to pump blood, but also to radiate forgiveness, mercy, love, compassion. It seems that your hearts only pump blood, as we see on the TV screens. Is that right?"

'The Palestinians, I think, have lost hope, and many of them consider that to die is better than to continue living, because if you are daily humiliated, if you are continually in a prison called a town or village, it is extremely depressing. On the other side, the Jews are also very, very scared. They don't know when they can go out and come back safe. All these "kamikazes" who explode themselves expressing their hopelessness are scaring the Jews to death. I hope one day our Jewish friends will wake up to see that the reason for all this insecurity is the perpetuation of occupation. Palestinians do not hate – it's not innate hatred, but Palestinians are cornered so badly that they kick back and kill themselves. They have had enough of being humiliated. For 55 years they have been cornered.

'The Jews need liberation; the Palestinians need liberation. The Jews from their own fear, from their own trauma, from their own greed to possess the whole land, and the Palestinians need to be free to circulate between their towns and villages and to feel that their land also belongs to them. We must stop the vicious circle; our life is becoming a kind of procession of funerals on both sides.'

## The witness of the protest marches – 'you have saved our lives'

Elias went on, 'It seems that the powers of the United States and England still believe that whenever they have enough weapons, they can impose any rule they want, not only in Afghanistan, not only in Iraq – if you suspect that someone will grow up to make weapons, kill him before he grows up! It's the law of the jungle, and that's why our hope, as Palestinian Christians, is rather in the Christianity of the West, the Christianity that stood so courageously, saying "No" to the war, "No" to the violence.

'I think that the anti-war protests in England, in Europe and in America, constitute for us a kind of guarantee for the survival of the 15 million Arab Christians in the Middle East. Otherwise, if these protest marches had not happened, we would have been identified with President Bush, who went on a crusade, and with Blair, who followed him blindly; and we would have been affiliated with those kinds of Christians. But they don't speak the language of Jesus Christ; Jesus Christ never spoke the language – "who is not with me is evil, we have to suffocate them, to kill them, to flush them out" – my goodness, this is not Christian. He spoke about forgiveness: while he was hanging on the cross he had the courage to say, "Father, they're idiots, they don't know what they do, forgive them." And we don't have that in international political speech today, which is why you Christians of the West, who have the courage to stand up in the streets and say "no" to the war, you have saved our lives, we the Palestinian Christians, and we the Arab Christians in the Middle East.'

# Thursday: Ascension Day on the Mount of Olives

Acts 1.9–12

When he had said this, as they were watching, he was lifted up, and a cloud took him out of their sight. While he was going and they were gazing up towards heaven, suddenly two men in white robes stood by them. They said, 'Men of Galilee, why do you stand looking up towards heaven?' ... Then they returned to Jerusalem from the mount called Olivet, which is near Jerusalem.

It is Ascension Day so we are back in Jerusalem. The traditional site of the Ascension in Jerusalem is the Mosque or Church of the Ascension, on the Mount of Olives. It was not open when we arrived but a ring on the bell seems to bring someone to open up fairly swiftly. The first Ascension church was built on this site around 394. Prior to that, Jerusalem Christians remembered the Ascension in a cave on the Mount of Olives. The Byzantine church was symbolically open to the sky, and the Crusaders maintained this when they built the church that is there now, which they built in an octagonal shape. In 1198 Saladin turned it into a mosque, putting a dome on the top and adding a *mihrab*, and it has been one ever since. Though it is not mentioned in the Koran, Muslims believe that Jesus ascended to heaven. There are rings round the edge of the walls of the compound for pitching tents on the feast of the Ascension, when Armenians, Copts, Greek Orthodox, Latin Catholic and Syrian churches are all allowed to celebrate Mass.

Our guide on this day round Jerusalem was Wisam's friend and former lecturer, Rimon Maklouf, a Jerusalemite himself. (He was the one singing in Aramaic in our visit earlier to the Syriac church.) The Maklouf family have lived for 400 years in the Old City. His father was in the Jerusalem police during British Mandate times, and their house was destroyed by the Irgun and Haganah in 1948. He pointed out that land is being taken and houses demolished all the time in East Jerusalem. Intriguingly, he said that as well as Christians in his family there are Muslims and Jews, which shows something of the good relationships in earlier times.

How should we respond to the Ascension? I asked two 'men of Galilee' about their thoughts on this and they give us the clues to our response. First, Fuad Dagher.

## Go and do something

'Ascension has to do with the message of the two angels who appeared to the disciples while they were looking up towards heaven – the words broke through their silence, their fear, their anxiety, and those looks which were saying "What are we going to do now?" And the angels said, "Why are you standing looking up to heaven? Go and do something, for God's sake, why are you frozen? It's time for you to do something" – and that is the challenge to the Church – "for God's sake, stop standing looking to heaven and doing nothing. It's time for you to work."'

## A Church for all

'It's time for the leaders of the Church to work more on the issues of peace and justice. The message of Jesus Christ is the message of justice and reconciliation, of dignity and respect for all humankind. Jesus did not work with a certain group, leaving another group; Jesus is a man of all groups. I don't want to be looked upon as a Church for a certain group – we are a Church for all groups, for all humankind. Therefore Ascension is a strong message: go on, do something. It's your turn, complete the work, and you are not by yourselves. The one who said to you, "Go and preach," also said to you, "I will be with you until the end of the world" – the same person. We have the Holy Spirit, we are equipped. So this is the message of the Ascension, and that's how I see it in terms of our situation – go on, it's now your time to work. We should not leave it to the leaders of the world to do this task; it's our task as a Church – we are the losers if we leave it to the leaders of the world. The leaders of the world have the weapons of the world; we have the weapons of God in our hands as a Church.'

So Fuad reminds us to 'get up and do something'. I then spoke to Elias Chacour, mentioning that the Ascension could be hard to understand. He put it in context.

## The icons of Christ

'After the Resurrection we were not able to relate to the Lord as we related before his Resurrection. Before, he was a man living with us, feeling with us, suffering with us, sleeping, eating, doing everything – now that he has been in glory, we are not allowed to relate to him physically. In order to see him well, you have to close your eyes, and we have two ways to see the Lord, two places; one way is to close your eyes, go deep into your heart, and remember that you are created in the image and likeness of God. And the other way is to look left and right, at those who are sitting with you, and remember that they are the icons of God, or the icons of Christ who is the icon of God. So the

Ascension was this event that helped the disciples to cross from living with the man from Galilee to relate to the Son of God who was that man of Galilee.'

## Friday: The God of the sheer silence

1 Kings 19.11–13

He said, 'Go out and stand on the mountain before the LORD, for the LORD is about to pass by.' Now there was a great wind, so strong that it was splitting mountains and breaking rocks in pieces before the LORD, but the LORD was not in the wind; and after the wind an earthquake, but the LORD was not in the earthquake; and after the earthquake a fire, but the LORD was not in the fire; and after the fire a sound of sheer silence. When Elijah heard it, he wrapped his face in his mantle and went out and stood at the entrance of the cave.

I had not visited Shehadeh Shehadeh, the vicar of St John's in Haifa, since my first book; it was time to return. Haifa is the third biggest city in Israel, it is very busy and seems to keep its charms somewhat hidden. I was with Khalil Harouny and we decided to go up to Stella Maris first and visit one of the caves associated with Elijah, a place of significance for Muslim, Jew and Christian.

We went to the cave next to the Carmelite monastery which Napoleon had used as a hospital for his troops when attacking Akko. Elijah is also called Mar Elias, and the Muslims associate him with Al-Khader – somehow they get combined. At the far end of the cave there are little pieces of paper pushed in the gaps in the wall, like the Western Wall in Jerusalem. Frankly, I found it a place to take a look and meditate on the folly of Elijah and his wrong use of power. Interfaith dialogue with Elijah was conducted with a sword, and this was how he understood the nature of God. Having killed the prophets of Baal, he came to somewhere like this cave. Interestingly, God gives exhibitions of power, but God is not in the power; God is in the 'sheer silence', perhaps the silence of despair at all that had happened in the name of God. When we need to re-establish balance in our lives, it is the silence that can be a help, a place of encounter with God and therefore a place of refreshment.

Next we headed down to Wadi Nisnas, the Arab quarter of Haifa, and found our way to St John's to meet up with Shehadeh. I asked him first about St John's School.

## St John's School and Church, Haifa

'We have about 420 children. We have an elementary school, and we have a pre-kindergarten, from 3 years old to 14 years old, to eighth grade. We have our peace programme, and all students, including Muslims and Christians of all denominations, go to the chapel once a day and listen to a sermon; usually I talk about ethics, behaviour, peace and how to make dialogue with people.'

I asked Shehadeh next about St John's Church and how many there are in the congregation: 'About 300 – we were a much larger community in 1948, but most of our congregation left, and what was left here was less than 200, and that has grown to be about 300 now.' I asked him how long he has lived in Haifa and how life is for the Christian community:

91

'I grew up in Galilee, I come from a small village in the Galilee called Kafr Yasif, and I lived in that village until I was 18, then I left for my higher studies. I served for a short while in the West Bank, in Nablus and Ramallah, but most of my time has been spent in the Galilee, in Haifa and Kafr Yasif and Shefa'Amr. The situation for the Christian population in this area is hard; the numbers are dwindling. Even the natural increase of the Christians in this area is less than any other group in Israel. So we are getting less and less and many Christians are leaving the country for a better situation; "We live only once," many people say, "and let's move away instead of being under pressure all the time and worrying about the future of our children." There is a lot of discrimination against the whole Arab community, and the Christians also, because they are part of the Palestinian community in Israel. The first question they ask you if you apply for a job is, "Did you serve in the army?" So the army is the key; and we don't serve in the army – nobody asks us to serve in the army, Israel doesn't want us to serve in the army, and at the same time they demand service in the army.'

## Message to Christians

'What I want to say to Christians who come and visit this area, I wish they'd come and visit us also, not just the old places. It's very important for them, I'm sure, that they want to see the places where Jesus walked, but we are the "living stones", we are the people who are still keeping these holy places, and we don't want to remain here as only the keepers of these places. My wish is that they would come and learn more about us, and talk with us about our situation; and we would learn more about them, so that we could be one Church – one united Church.'

## Final thoughts about Haifa

'Haifa is very well known for its good co-existence between Jews and Palestinians, although we live in two separate quarters, but we live in understanding and quiet; we respect each other. A number of us support all kinds of programmes to make this come true, and to gather both Jews and Palestinians, to talk, to listen, to understand, and to accept the other person. Amram Mitznah (previous Mayor of Haifa, and unsuccessful leader of the Labour party in the spring 2003 election) was one of those persons who supported such a move. All the time he visited the whole community, he used to come to me once a year, at least. I used to meet him in several locations all through the year. He is a nice person, and I hope there will be many people like him in the Jewish area and in the Palestinian area, so that we could really start doing programmes to accept each other.'

## Saturday: A Muslim voice in Akko

Surah 2.153 (Koran)
O ye who truly believe, seek your strength for defeating injustice and oppression in your steadfastness and prayers. Assuredly, God is on the side of the steadfast in truth.

### 'When a Jewish soldier dies I cry too'

Akko is an interesting place to visit, especially to see the subterranean Crusader city and the Khan al-Umdan Caravanserai, but this time I only wanted to visit the

Mosque of Al Jezzar and St George's Orthodox Church. At the mosque I got chatting with Abu Mohammed, who was sitting just inside the gate, and he proved to have a lot of earthy wisdom; I enjoyed our chat. I asked him for his views and he said:

'Everyone, Christian and Muslim, should respect each other as a human being. There are no problems between Arabs and Jews – 1948 is the problem. One group was taken and thrown out and another group brought in. But,' he said, 'the problem can be fixed; let the Palestinian refugees return and people will live together.

'America is the strongest country in the world and does what she likes, and takes no notice of the UN. As a human being I don't like this and what you've done to Iraq.' Knowing I was British, he asked, 'Why is Blair following America without thinking? They've come to take the oil; they want to be rulers of the whole world.

'As human beings we like the US and Britain – they are kind but as rulers they are against Muslims. They want to make peace when the problem in the Middle East is not fixed by only taking the side of Israel. When you want to be a judge you must be a straight judge. When a Jewish soldier dies I cry too – he has a mother, and I'm a religious man. So stop killing and let's make peace – you have to leave the Occupied Territories, because you're sitting inside my house. Please, my dear friends and dear humans, study very well the Muslim religion; Islam is when you give all yourself to God and build for the next life. So don't love money – be a good friend to God and be a good human being. I pray for all human beings, even those who don't believe in God.'

### A message to Tony Blair

He then sent a rather moving message to the Prime Minister. 'Mr Tony Blair – you're not going to be Prime Minister so long, but you will still be a human being. Let the people love you, not hate you. Be straight so they love you. So many women in Iraq have lost sons and children, and, Mr Blair, you are the reason. If you had said "no" to Bush maybe he would have stopped.'

Abu Mohammed had a lovely smile – we shook hands and I went away pondering on how well the 'Arab street' understands what is happening in the world, and has a moral and spiritual response. I went and had a look in the mosque; it is very beautiful with white writing from the Koran picked out against blue. It was in the process of being redecorated.

We headed on to St George's Orthodox Church (1845). It was locked, but Khalil said we could probably meet the priest. He too was in the middle of redecorating (it was obviously the season) but he was very hospitable and stopped to chat. He was Archimandrite Philotheos (an Archimandrite is like the superior of a monastery), and has responsibility for the Church in Akko, and represents the Patriarch, the Archbishop of Ptolemais Pallarius, Metropolitan of Ptolemais and Western Galilee, when he is not in the country. He has spent three years in Akko, and he told me there are 1,500 Christians in Akko, which has a population of around 70,000.

He said that Russian immigrants come to the church and they baptize their children. They write to the Ministry of the Interior about this, because conversion is not allowed, but 'don't get much in the way of an answer. Actually it only applies if they have "Jewish faith" on their ID – if they have no faith then they don't have to apply for permission.'

'But,' he went on, 'the main focus of the church is Arab Orthodox. This community has direct contact with Jesus Christ; maybe their ancestors ate of the five loaves and the two fish, and they drank the wine at Cana of Galilee. In Western Galilee there are around 30,000 Christians in the Greek Orthodox Church; it is called the Metropolis of Ptolemais (the Romans called Akko Ptolemais). In St George's Church in Akko about 40 to 50 come normally, but many more on a feast day.' I asked Philotheos about St George; he said that 25 February is their St George's Day. He was clear also about the symbolism of the myth: 'The dragon is the devil, and the daughter of the king is the Church.'

Philotheos summed up by saying, 'We pray for peace but it is not comfortable to see Jenin and Nablus and Gaza attacked by Apache helicopters and tanks. We pray to Jesus Christ for peace, prosperity and love, and we call on people to come as pilgrims; we need them for the life of Palestine.' As a parting shot I asked him his view on the Trinity – there is something rather wonderful about tossing a huge issue like that to someone, an issue over which the Church has grappled for centuries. Philotheos (his name means 'one who loves God') was unfazed, and I was shocked that he responded with almost a soundbite, 'One God with three faces', and that was it.

## Prayer

This week, O God, we have walked 'towards the dawn', learning not only from people's struggles, but also hearing the call to 'do something – it's our turn'. We all need liberation, we all need to discover our own humanity by discovering it in others. We all need to discover our response to 'do something'. Help us to discover, God, what we can do, how we should respond. Amen.

# WEEK 5: FROM NAZARETH TO CAPERNAUM

## Sunday: Nazareth wanderings

Luke 2.39–40
When they had finished everything required by the law of the Lord, they returned to Galilee, to their own town of Nazareth. The child grew and became strong, filled with wisdom; and the favour of God was upon him.

A stroll in Nazareth is rewarding. Many tours rush through and see very little and meet no locals. So stay for a few days, as it is a good place to be based to visit Galilee and have a day or two to wander in Nazareth itself. For an interesting tour, start at the Church of the Annunciation, a remarkable modern building covering a rock cave which has been venerated since the third century as the house of Mary. It has large striking murals from around the world and beautiful bronze doors featuring events in the life of Jesus.

Then a visit to St Joseph's Church next door is interesting. It was built in 1914 on the site of a twelfth-century church; under the church there are caves, granaries and wells used by early dwellers in Nazareth. It used to be claimed that this was the site of the carpenter's workshop. It has lovely paintings, one of Joseph with Jesus and another in the carpenter's workshop. It is rather refreshing to see Joseph featured. Next, head into the market, up to the Greek Orthodox church with the little synagogue next to it – perhaps built over the one Jesus would have visited. Not far away is Christ Church Anglican church, which is very beautiful inside. Later we will talk to the vicar, Samuel Barhoum.

Now, head down the high street until you come to Mazzawi's souvenir shop on the left. It is a place of very good-quality products, selling a whole range of items including some remarkable icons. The Mazzawis are a very friendly Christian family. Naim Mazzawi works here with his father and other family members. I have known him for many years, since he came to the Greenbelt Festival at the turn of the 1990s with the Christ Church youth group. He talked to me about the current pressures on them all.

## Painful truth from Naim

'At present it is a very hard situation. It has been this way for three years. For our family, as with many others, our lives and our work are based on tourism. At the end of every tunnel is a light, but we don't see this light. It's hard to be optimistic. So we are suffering a lot as Christians in the Holy Land, living in a double minority, but we have a faith. We are believers, and we say whatever happens we know there should be a light, if not on this earth, it will be up there, and this is what makes us strong. I belong to a Greek Catholic church; our church is situated in the old market, right next to the synagogue. All my life I have been going there, since I was five or six years old, because of my father, he is a very strong believer, so we grew up in his footsteps.

'From the point of view of an Israeli Palestinian

Christian living in Israel as a citizen it is very difficult. I think there is a lack of knowledge about Christians living in the Holy Land, but we are original Christians, going back 2,000 years to Jesus Christ. There should be an introduction to us – we are about 2 per cent today of the population of Israel; we need pilgrims to come here and support us, whether financially, whether spiritually or with prayers. I ask them to come and stay in Nazareth – don't just spend one hour.'

## October 2000

'In October 2000 we had a great shock, because 13 people were killed in Nazareth. As Israeli citizens we should have equal rights whether we are Arabs or Jewish. So we didn't expect Israeli forces, whether police or army, to shoot Arab citizens, living in their state. What happened here was done on purpose, they wanted to give a message to the citizens, that they would kill, on purpose. This was a very painful thing to have happened in Israel – like a glass, when it's broken, it's broken. You can never glue pieces of glass together again, so this has created something wrong between us; now there are two groups of civilians in Israel, Arabs and Jews.'

## 'This is not life'

'This is not life here. We are struggling every day and we want to live life in a peaceful way, we want to enjoy life, and we don't enjoy it.'

It was hard to hear that times are so hard that the Christians of Nazareth will not survive unless groups go back and support them. Naim, who is always so full of life and sparkle, had taken a battering, like everyone in Nazareth.

## To the shrine of temptation

On your Nazareth pilgrimage, after visiting Mazzawi's turn around as if going back to the Church of the Annunciation, stopping only at Suheil Fathi Said's curiously named 'Chick's Fried Chicken' shop for a falafel or schwarma in pitta bread! For the second course, go on to Mahroum's Mid-East sweet and cake shop on the left further down the road, which is truly a site of temptation. Here since 1890 unwary pilgrims have been lured in to eat sticky delicacies. I have found myself enticed here repeatedly. They make 20 different types of oriental flavoured sweets and delicacies, such as Baklawa, Kataife, Zenobia's Fingers, Nightingales' Nests and Lukum. I am not sure which is which, but I like to sample widely to make sure nothing is left out! It is part café, so a cup of tea with the cakes is pure joy. You can be relieved to know that they are all made with natural ingredients and are chemical free – you are, however, half a stone heavier afterwards.

So, reluctantly and more slowly, now it is time to move on from Mahroum's, taking the right-hand fork to Mary's Well. The building is relatively new, only three or four years old, but the taps have been removed and frankly at present it is all rather disappointing. This is because the spring has become polluted and vandals have spoiled it, but this is not actually the source of the water – this is in the church behind, St Gabriel's. This very beautiful church is the Orthodox Church of the Annunciation. Here, at the far end of the church, you can drink from the spring, which is believed to have healing properties. You can also spend time quietly meditating on the striking paintings on walls and ceiling, and the hand-made wooden iconostasis. There is a very beautiful pulpit with what looks at first glance like a chicken on top, but it turns out to be the eagle representing St John.

Outside (where there is an olive tree, for some reason growing in a cart), take the right fork and go back by a different route. It will eventually lead you back to St Joseph's and the old market where your journey began.

An excellent place to stay in Nazareth is St Margaret's Pilgrim Hostel run by the Anglican Church, which you can walk up to from the old market. It is an extremely steep walk but this exercise may be good if the stop in Mahroum's went on too long! St Margaret's has some of the best views in Nazareth, looking right across to the plain of Megiddo. It has a very attractive courtyard, which is welcoming and relaxing and a lovely place to return to in the evenings.

## Monday: 'We long to be considered equal'

Micah 6.6–8
What does the LORD require of you but to do justice, and to love kindness, and to walk humbly with your God?

Each evening at St Margaret's, groups from the parish would be popping in for meetings, often with the vicar, Samuel Barhoum. Samuel and Susan asked me to their house for a meal one evening, which gave me the ideal chance to interview them (Susan on Wednesday next week). I asked Samuel about Holy Family Church and the Christians of Reineh. He told me they have about 200 people in the church (in Reineh the population is 40,000 and 20 per cent are Christians): 'We have four churches – the Anglican church, the Latin or Catholic church, the Greek Orthodox church, and the Melkite (Greek Catholic) church.'

I asked him for his reflections on life in Galilee. He said, 'As a Palestinian Christian who lives in Israel, we have a very complicated identity. We are Christians, we are Palestinians, we are Arabs, we are Israelis by citizenship; we have to live with this situation, and in these days, when I talk to people, many have no hope for peace and no hope for a better life. So many are thinking of emigration, especially young adults and young couples. For example, in my young adult group in my parish here in Reineh, three of them are now outside the country – they emigrated last summer.

'We are seeking human rights. We want to be equals with the others here; to be in a country that is for all its citizens, this is what we are seeking. We want to be considered equal to the Jewish person who came to this land several years ago, maybe a couple of years ago, and yet is a full citizen and I am less than a second-class citizen and experience discrimination. Now we are thinking of a new idea, which Knesset member Azmi Bishara suggested: we want a country for all its citizens, all equal, like anybody who lives in England – a full citizen, with all the rights of a citizen. God is justice; so do you believe that God will love you more than me, or will love a Jewish person more than me? It is not justice.'

## 'We feel forsaken. Are we still your sisters and brothers in Christ?'

'I want to say to pilgrims and tourists: ask about the Christians who live in the Holy Land, worship with us, spend time with us. Tell others about us, and encourage them to come over. In my parish, we used to have many groups who came to our congregation, and they stayed with us in our homes for a couple of nights. Now they are very good friends of ours. Since 11 September nobody comes, especially not from the US. Yesterday I was with the Bishop of Massachusetts and he asked me when I saw the last Anglican bishop come to the Holy Land; I told him, "It was you, last year." I asked him what they think as Americans about Palestinian Christians. Are we still your sisters and brothers in Christ? I and all the parishioners feel that we are forsaken. If people would organize pilgrimages where they come to different churches and spend time with people, that would bring encouragement.'

### 'We are not flies – we are human beings'

'Politically they have come out with the road map. I don't know if you have read this road map, but what about the Palestinians who live in Israel? Nobody mentions us. From the beginning, from Oslo until now, nobody has said a word about us. We are not moving to the West Bank because we belong to Galilee, we are rooted here. So what about mentioning us and giving full citizenship for the Palestinians who live in Israel? If you say this country is only for a specific people it is a racist thing. What about the people who were here before 1948? We are not bees, we are not flies, we are human beings. What about us? They have forgotten about us. If there will be the State of Israel beside the State of Palestine, that will be all right for everybody, but give rights to the Palestinians in Israel and to Jewish people in Palestine.'

# Tuesday: The White Mosque

'A thief is closer to God and more beloved by people than those who by faith and religion devour others – who make religion like commerce.' (Ali Ibn Abi Talim, cousin of the Prophet Muhammad; on the wall of the White Mosque in Nazareth)

## *Peace and fraternity among all*

There is a well-known lithograph of Nazareth by David Roberts on his journey to Palestine in 1838–9, in which one of the outstanding features is the White Mosque. It is still there today, now 300 years old and the most ancient mosque in Nazareth. The Haram (praying place) was built first, in 1785, then the arcade and minaret.

Khalil arranged for me to meet Atef Yousuf Al-Fahoum, who is custodian of the mosque and owns the trust that looks after it. As Khalil and I stood waiting for prayers to end, he explained to me that as the people came out they would say, '*Assalam aleikum*' ('Peace be upon you'), and I should reply, '*Waleikum assalam*'; a few moments later we were indeed being greeted by everyone. On the board outside, the message of the mosque is 'peace and fraternity among all communities'.

## *Muslim voices*

We went in and spoke with Atef Al-Fahoum. He was warm, welcoming and dignified and full of fascinating information. He started off, as everyone did at this time, by speaking of the world situation and said that the US is controlling the world by slogans. He went on to say that the Anglo-American war against Iraq was not fair, and the attitude against Arab nations was not fair. He said, 'God doesn't give the US and the English a special message to lead the world or control others. It is not fair to say "might is right". We all want to live in peace and harmony – I'm not to be controlled because of oil or other reasons. I like to be in good co-operation with all nations, to make it a good new world, to give a chance to all to live without any differences and in peace.'

He had sent messages from the White Mosque to the White House, to ask them to 'strengthen peace, justice, and humanity, among nations, and oppressed minorities in the whole world'. Atef said of the Anglo-American alliance, 'They said the Iraqi government had weapons of mass destruction but they found nothing – they should be shy.' It was rather a nice turn of phrase; it would indeed be a welcome change to see a government being shy! He pointed out that the White Mosque was built by his ancestor Abdullah Al-Fahoum, and has been run ever since by a family trust or Waqf. He is the tenth custodian and has been the trustee for 34 years. He feels a responsibility to keep implementing the mosque's message of peace and teaching true Islam as a religion of peace and tolerance.

His father was elected Mayor of Nazareth in the Second World War. When Partition came in November 1947, most people fled, expecting to come back soon, and took their keys. Now, over 55 years later, they are left without any hope. His father understood the UN decision. He sensed that as they had taken most of the country he should make peace, so his father asked people to stay and make an agreement between Jews and Arabs. He made the first Arab/Jewish agreement with Chaim Laskov on 16

July 1948; this agreement was basically a surrender, but it avoided the bloodshed that other places experienced. (Under the UN Partition Plan of 1947, Nazareth should have been part of the Arab state of Palestine.)

### 'We must love the Jews'

Talking further about the current situation, Atef said, 'I like to see negotiations, not fighting. Arab powers cannot fight against Israel (which is the West) so we must love the Jews – love is greater. I am 73 years old; I know Israel from the beginning. There is one policy – whether left or right there is no difference – they are working for the benefit of the state. My message would be that we hope that very soon we can live together in harmony, with Arabs and Jews having rights and living together and making peace. Most of my friends are Christians; I don't differentiate, nor with Jews. I only differentiate between good and bad; our blood is the same – we are all human beings.'

Taking us round the mosque, Atef pointed out that 'Islam is Salaam (peace)'. He then made us stand in line in the way people do at prayers, saying, 'They line up when praying because people are equal like teeth on a comb.'

## Wednesday: Meeting Adalah

Luke 6.43–45
No good tree bears bad fruit, nor again does a bad tree bear good fruit; for each tree is known by its own fruit. Figs are not gathered from thorns, nor are

grapes picked from a bramble bush. The good person out of the good treasure of the heart produces good ... for it is out of the abundance of the heart that the mouth speaks.

## Jewish voices: Orna Kohn

Galilee has a romantic ring for many Christian pilgrims; it means stillness by the Sea of Galilee. It means that for me; but it also means people, and the more you meet them the more the Galilee story they tell you reminds you of a deep spiritual truth. Jesus tells the disciples to go back to Galilee where they will see him. And we do see Jesus in Galilee, not in some romanticized spirituality but in the daily struggles of a suffering community. We cannot pretend that all is well in Galilee – we cannot pass these people by on the other side. Over 400 villages have been destroyed in the last 55 years, and there are still people living in unrecognized villages with no facilities after all this time. But there are also those committed to bringing justice and hope to the community.

One example of this is Jewish lawyer Orna Kohn, who works for Adalah (Justice) legal centre serving the Arab community. Their main goal is to achieve equality and minority rights protection for Arab citizens of Israel in land and housing, education, employment, language, culture, in political rights, women's rights, prisoners' rights and religious rights. I asked Orna to explain the work:

'Adalah is a legal centre for human rights. We deal mainly with the institutional discrimination of the Arab minority in Israel. But since April 2002 during the invasion, NGOs in Gaza and the West Bank were unable to function, because the Israeli army took over their offices, arrested their lawyers, and there was no ability for these organizations to act in any way. We were asked by them to help. So we went to the High Court on different issues, including the house demolitions in Jenin at the time that it happened. Once the human rights organizations in the West Bank were able to start re-functioning we pulled back, but we still deal with human shield cases – the fact that the Israeli army is using civilians as shields in order to be able to arrest people or demolish houses.

'But our focus is the Arab minority in Israel, and we are dealing with many aspects: like the effects of the shootings in Nazareth in October 2000 – the 13 people who were killed by the Israeli police. This has been a major focus of our work for the last two and a half years; we have been representing the families of the 13. We are just waiting for the final report of the committee to come out. There are many similarities to Bloody Sunday, not only that 13 were killed, but I am afraid that we will also need a second committee. I think in many ways the report that is about to be published is going to have many silences and be blaming the victims, and I think very little truth will come out in it.

'I have been working for Adalah now for five years, and one of my cases is the issue of family reunification. We have already been dealing with many cases of violations of the rights of families to be united – of Arab citizens in Israel who are married to a spouse from the West Bank or Gaza. There were always many cases, and for years I was able to advocate for them before the ministry. For years we received many sweets from people who got a status (temporary status) through us, and were extremely happy. And suddenly, from March 2002, all these people are back in my office, because the status that they had suddenly could not be renewed. In March 2002, the interior ministry ordered a freeze on all family unification requests if at least one of the couple was a Palestinian or an Arab. In May 2002, I had a case and I was about to go to court, and the Israeli government ruled in favour of a decision saying that from now on, when one of the spouses is Palestinian, they will be treated differently from other family reunification cases. There is the Law of Return, which means that any Jew who wants to come to Israel is entitled to come automatically with spouse, children, grandchildren and their spouses. At the same time, citizenship laws concerning the Arab minority in Israel are some of the most restricting in Western countries. We're starting to work with Amnesty International on it, but I really think that we will need to bring this issue to very high attention of the international community.'

Just as I was writing up this section, the Knesset passed a law preventing Palestinians who marry Israeli Arabs from living in Israel. They must leave or live apart. Human rights organizations immediately denounced this as racist and undemocratic. The front page headline in the *Independent* on 1 August was 'Israel imposes "racist" marriage law'. Amnesty International and Human Rights Watch both wrote to the Knesset about it, and Amnesty released a statement that this clearly violates 'international human rights laws and treaties which Israel has ratified and pledged to uphold'.

Orna and Adalah were quoted in the *Guardian* of the same day; Adalah's statement pointed out that it is 'racist' because it applies only to Palestinian spouses, and Orna said, 'It's shocking, not only because it's so severe but because it came from the government. In the past there were similar attempts to pass similar bills but that was done by the extreme right wing.' Once again there is 'naught for your comfort' here.

## Palestinian victims in Israel

Orna commented: 'The Palestinians in Israel, the Arab minority, are the forgotten Palestinians. People know about the Palestinian refugees in Lebanon – they know of course about Gaza and the West Bank – but then there is Israel, the Jewish state. The fact that a fifth of its population are the original residents of this country, who managed to stay in 1948, is quite a new and shocking piece of information to many. And part of it is because if it's a Jewish state, how can it be that you have such a big national minority, who are not immigrants, and the state can still be Jewish? If there was no occupation in the West Bank and Gaza, then the story of the Palestinians in Israel would be a very high priority to the international community, because the kind of human rights violations we have here are terrible.'

# Thursday: 'We believe in humanity'

Matthew 5.9
Blessed are the peacemakers, for they will be called the children of God.

Proverbs 9.10
The fear of the LORD is the beginning of wisdom, and the knowledge of the Holy One is insight.

The first thing I ever did in Nazareth on my first visit to the town was to go and sing to the pupils of Christ Church School, who sang back to me with a beauty and power that I found very moving. Since then, the school has developed in remarkable ways and continues to do so. Education is very important to the Palestinian community of Israel – they do not get the same facilities and opportunities, so a school that offers them the best is very significant, not just for education but also for dignity.

The headmaster is Hanna Abu El-Assal, the son of Bishop Riah. He is a relentless enthusiast and entrepreneur, an ideal new style of management headmaster full of ideas and passionate concern that the Israeli Palestinian community, who have been treated for so long as second best, should now have the best facilities in education and the best chances possible. He wants his community to be treated with dignity, and he is proud of what the school has achieved and the attitude of the students. The school is next door to St Margaret's Pilgrim Hostel, so we went to see how it had developed and to meet up with Hanna. He was as irrepressible as ever, and we had a most entertaining look round the school, which included a little bit of learning for me on Maths in one classroom.

He filled us in on the latest developments at the school: 'The school has doubled in numbers and reputation. When I started in 1993/94 we had 210 students; this year we have 1,040. Next year I am expecting 1,200 students. They come from as many as 31 villages and different towns in Galilee – some even travel for an hour to get here. Now we have two elementary schools, and two kindergartens and one high school. We have just named the high school after Bishop Riah: you will probably have seen the inscription at the front of the school.' (It has the words of Matthew 5.9 on it.)

'In September 2001 we opened a new building, and all the classes are well equipped with computers and videos. We have recently opened a new science laboratory, and in October we will open the new library. My father's dream is to have a college or university here as well, and we are getting close to that becoming a reality.'

### 'We believe in humanity'

'The most important thing we believe in is humanity. We don't care if the student is a Christian or a Muslim or a Jew. We stress that we are all equal, we are all human beings. One of the most important aspects of the school as well as education is behaviour. We have taught our students to live together as human beings, as family, and that we are all parts of the same body.'

At the end of our tour round the school we came to a beautiful olive tree planted in the school playground with some words in Arabic script on a piece of stone. Hanna told us it was words from Proverbs 9.10, 'The fear of the LORD is the beginning of wisdom.'

Hanna's enthusiasm is infectious, and we left there encouraged that so many pupils will not only get an excellent education but see a way to live that treats them with respect, so in turn they can treat others with respect. This is peacemaking at a very deep level.

## Friday: A day by the Sea of Galilee

Matthew 11.20–30

Then he began to reproach the cities in which most of his deeds of power had been done, because they did not repent. 'Woe to you ... And you, Capernaum, will you be exalted to heaven? No ... Come to me, all you that are weary and are carrying heavy burdens, and I will give you rest. Take my yoke upon you, and learn from me; for I am gentle and humble in heart, and you will find rest for your souls. For my yoke is easy, and my burden is light.'

Capernaum was to become Jesus' adopted home. It is now assumed that he lived in Peter's house, and recent excavations have found the names of Peter and Jesus scribbled on the walls by early Jewish believers. It was from here that Jesus started his travels, and it became the base for his ministry and is referred to twice as 'his own town' (Matthew 9.1 and Mark 2.1). Most pilgrim groups seem to come to visit Capernaum, and come to see the remains of Peter's house and the nearby synagogue. The house remains are from the right period and though obviously nothing can be proved, the extent of early respect seems to give this a good degree of authenticity. The synagogue, though, comes from the third or fourth century.

When here I have always found myself peering across to the very attractive Greek Orthodox Church of All Apostles just down the shore, with its little red turrets or domes, and at last on this trip I got to visit it. It had to be opened specially, and it was like entering a secret garden. It seems to be part garden and part smallholding. It is well worth bringing a group here, first to take a look inside the very beautiful church with its lovely paintings, then simply for the stillness of the setting by the lake. It is a place to sit for a while to recollect that somewhere near here Jesus walked and framed his thinking and made his prayers.

We were the only visitors and so Brother Erinarchos, who lives here, came and welcomed us and made us coffee. He has been here since 1987 and we spent time talking – he was very amusing and informative. He told us that there is a big festival on 12 July (the feast of St Peter and St Paul) when they bless the lake, which is drinking-water for all Israel. He likes to point out to authorities that they are drinking holy water! Then he told us about the church and its services; every month on a Saturday a service is held for new Russian immigrants – the church is normally full, with 200–300 on a holy day. Russian immigrants are also baptized here – babies inside the church and adults in the lake.

## The non-violence of Jesus

The Bible passage above is a curious mixture of judgement and comfort. Jack Nelson-Pallmeyer calls for us to embrace the non-violence of Jesus and be more critical of the violence that he feels is projected on to God by the writers of both the Old and the New Testaments. He says, 'Matthew builds on this association between Jesus and the wrath of God by presenting Jesus as an endtime judge associated with the "Son of Man", an apocalyptic figure ... Apocalypticism included the expectation of a new, decisive, and imminent violent coming of God to destroy the wicked and vindicate the good' (*Jesus against*

*Christianity*, Trinity Press International, 2001, pp. 61–2). He concludes that Jesus is missing from much of our Christianity because of 'our unwillingness to approach scripture critically . . . and our refusal to let go of traditional notions of God's power . . . Non-violent images of God guided Jesus, grounded his faith, and informed his actions as he exposed and countered a deadly spiral of violence. His revelation of a non-violent God and his invitation to abundant life rooted in the generosity of God offer us an alternative way to live . . .'

I find Nelson-Pallmeyer's comments very challenging, and they call, at least, for a significant discussion on these issues. All of us are self-censoring about what we take from the Bible, but we may need to be more conscious about this in the light of the violence that is now so dominant in our world; this is even being pursued by leaders who claim to be Christian, and not least because of the terrible legacy of violence in this Holy Land. Would a rediscovery of the character of Jesus and a more rigorous critique of our holy scriptures help us to pursue a more healing route for all?

After the judgement of the Matthew passage come the wonderfully liberating words that certainly affirm abundant life. 'Come to me, all you that are weary . . . and I will give you rest. Take my yoke upon you, and learn from me; for I am gentle and humble in heart, and you will find rest for your souls.' Actually, this is the Jesus we know and recognize, who walked by the Sea of Galilee, and gave us the wonderful teachings about the community of God on Mount Eremos in the Sermon on the Mount.

# Saturday: By the lake with Bishop Riah

Matthew 8.1, 5–13

... When he entered Capernaum, a centurion came to him, appealing to him and saying, 'Lord, my servant is lying at home paralysed, in terrible distress.' And he said to him, 'I will come and cure him.' The centurion answered, 'Lord, I am not worthy to have you come under my roof; but only speak the word, and my servant will be healed' ... When Jesus heard him, he was amazed ...

The tradition is that the centurion's house was where the Greek Orthodox church is now; if so, maybe the centurion had been observing Jesus from a distance and therefore came to have this remarkable confidence, so that when his servant was ill he came to find Jesus. Jesus is astounded as he was not finding such support from all the locals whether in Nazareth or in Capernaum. Perhaps part of the reason for this is because of Jesus' background and the way he was aligning himself to a different group.

Bargil Pixner is a Benedictine monk who has lived for many years at the Sea of Galilee and written a book called *With Jesus through Galilee* (Corazin, 1996). He believes that Jesus' family were part of the Natzorean clan and that they were influenced by the Essenes. He believes Jesus broke from his family on this, and looked more to the influence of the Pharisees; Pixner only sees the division between family and disciples being reconciled when Jesus was on the cross.

Not far from Capernaum, past Jesus' favourite hill, Mount Eremos, down at the bottom of the hill by the lake is the Church of the Multiplication; it is at the place of seven springs or Heptapegon, shortened to Tabgha. Once again there is an attractive modern church (1982) built over the spot where a fifth-century church had been. Indeed, parts of this church belong to the Byzantine one, including the exceptional mosaics. Right in front of the altar is the well-known mosaic of the bread and fish. There is a rock under the altar which tradition suggests is the place where the miracle of the feeding of the 5,000 took place.

Bishop Riah joined us at the Church of the Multiplication, and took us on a short walk to an altar by the lakeside where the Galilee parishes celebrate Pentecost in the open air, some even fishing during the service, apparently! This would be a wonderful place to celebrate with the local Christians. This area is known as Dalmanutha-Magadan.

### Mount of the Beatitudes

We then went up to the Mount of Beatitudes (Mount Eremos). As we arrived, an Israeli school group was there with two armed guards, a reminder of why we need the Sermon on the Mount. Since the fourth century, this has been known as the site of the Beatitudes. In the 1930s the famous architect Belluci built a church here. We met Sister Salvoterenia, who had been there for four years, having previously been at Jericho, Bethlehem, Jordan and Kafr Cana. She is there to welcome people, and said that the message of the place to the world is 'Peace – we want peace.'

*Prayer*

From Nazareth to Capernaum, to your favourite mountain, we have walked this week, Jesus, in the company of the 'living stones' of Galilee. We feel close to you, both in the places where you lived and in your followers who try to live your gospel of hope in difficult times. Their temptation is to leave, but their vocation is to stay. May we keep building friendships with them, so we can learn from them and bring them the support and encouragement that they need. Amen.

## Sunday: Learn the language of others

Acts 2.1–12

When the day of Pentecost had come, they were all together in one place. And suddenly from heaven there came a sound like the rush of a violent wind ... All of them were filled with the Holy Spirit ... And ... the crowd gathered and was bewildered, because each one heard them speaking in the native language of each. Amazed and astonished, they asked, 'Are not all these who are speaking Galileans? And how is it that we hear, each of us, in our own native language? Parthians, Medes, Elamites, and residents of Mesopotamia, Judea and Cappadocia, Pontus and Asia, Phrygia and Pamphylia, Egypt and the parts of Libya belonging to Cyrene, and visitors from Rome, both Jews and prose-lytes, Cretans and Arabs – in our own languages we hear them speaking about God's deeds of power.'

Now the disciples lose their fear and find their sense of direction, their motivation and their strength for the task. Let's hear from some Galilee disciples about Pentecost.

*Galilee voices*

*Abuna Elias Chacour: 'It is more powerful to be diverse'*
'When I look at our Christian situation today, I hardly

recognize the man from Galilee, Jesus Christ. I think he finds himself alien in many church communities. The day of Pentecost was the opposite of Babylon (Babel) – there, they spoke one language and nobody understood the other, and here they were from many languages and they understood each other. And Pentecost, the day of reception of the Holy Spirit, was really the opening, the breaking of the capsule of the chosen-ness of the privileged people; it's opening the arms to the Gentiles, saying, "But you are God's children." It is the pluralistic community that was invited back to the house of the Father, not despite their differences but with their differences, which became an enrichment rather than a risk. The difference became something beautiful. It is much more powerful to be diverse and find the same goal than to be copies of each other.'

## Fuad Dagher: 'Learn the language of others'

'Pentecost is the day when we celebrate what Jesus promised to give, which is the Holy Spirit. I think the key word in our Christian living is the Spirit. Pentecost is when all were given the chance to understand each other, and our problem in this world is that we are not able to understand the language of each other. Each one of us has his own language, and thinks that his language is the language which has to be imposed on everyone – whether it is the terms of terrorism, or the terms of peace, or the terms of reconciliation. So many languages, but be open to Pentecost so as to be able to understand the language of others. And it's time for people to understand the Arabic language; also the language of peace, of readiness to shake hands, of readiness to start again, the language of not looking back but looking forward. Pentecost is a strong

121

message to the Church and to the leaders of the world – be open to understand and to learn the language of others. That's Pentecost.'

*Samuel Barhoum: 'We are Christians from Pentecost'*
'Here in Reineh we celebrate Pentecost, Easter and Christmas together, the Eastern Churches and the Western Churches. So all the churches in this village celebrate Christmas on 25 December, and everybody will celebrate Easter with the Orthodox Church – so last week we had Pentecost. And we had a picnic – this is a tradition here, to go for a picnic and celebrate the Eucharist outside in the woods. So I mentioned about Pentecost, that we have to be proud, that we were the first people who were given the responsibility of establishing the Church, who were given the message to go and tell others about Jesus. I believe Pentecost was the establishment of the Church, and we are Christians from Pentecost; I told them in my sermon, "Tell the West, we evangelized you!" We are Christians from the beginning, and should be proud of this.'

So the pluralistic community, the learning community, the Pentecostal community, three images that complement one another that open our eyes to the significance of this new community: 'We were "stormed" with the Spirit of God, and he took all the bad ideas, all the previous ideas, all the prejudices . . .' (Elias Chacour). And so the establishment of the Church happened at Pentecost and everybody is invited; now the task is to make sure all are listened to, and that diversity is cherished.

# Monday: Let my prayer come before you

John 7.37–42
On the last day of the festival ... Jesus ... cried out,
'Let anyone who is thirsty come to me, and let the one
who believes in me drink. As the scripture has said,
"Out of the believer's heart shall flow rivers of living
water."' Now he said this about the Spirit ...

So the Spirit is strength for the journey and for the tasks
that need to be done. It is the 'living water' of today's
passage that refreshes our thirsty spirits. It removed the
disciples' fear; they had felt uncertain what to do, but now
the vision was renewed. And from waiting in fear they
now go out in courage to live and share the gospel around
the world. Today our pilgrimage continues in Jerusalem
not far from the Upper Room, heading slightly backwards
in the story of Jesus and the Church, but it gives us a
further insight into the life and character of Jesus from the
'Fifth Gospel'.

## St Peter in Gallicantu
On our walk round Jerusalem, from the Upper Room
(Cenacle) we went to St Peter in Gallicantu. This is a very
good place to go early in a pilgrimage to get an idea of
Jerusalem, as from here you get excellent views. It is a
useful place to arrive mid-morning for coffee, or at
lunchtime, as they have a little café and very good loos! It
is a modern church built over what is thought to be the
site of Caiaphas' house. It is on four levels; you enter at

the top level, which is the church. This has very beautiful pictures done on ceilings with small tile mosaics. Then down to the next level where it is thought Jesus was brought before Caiaphas for his trial in what would have been an open courtyard, and then put in a cell underneath. You can look down to where the cells would have been; now it is a place of prayer, beautifully built with large icons. It does feel like sacred space and there is a sense of prayer.

Then down again to what would have been the guard-room. This looks like a prison – maybe this was where Jesus was scourged Then finally down to the dungeon where you can certainly imagine Jesus being held. Again it feels like a place for meditation; they have a little lectern with Psalm 88 on it for you to read: 'O LORD, God of my salvation . . . I cry out in your presence, let my prayer come before you . . . I am . . . like those forsaken among the dead.' On the way out there is a moving sculpture en-titled *The Servant of the Lord*, which shows Jesus kneeling with his hands bound. Next to it is a plaque with two passages, one from Isaiah 53 and the other from Philippians 2; this is the profound passage about Jesus taking the form of a servant and humbling himself to the point of death so God 'gave him a name above every name'.

Head outside the church to look at a lovely view of the Old City. It is a great place to chat and look at the walls of Jerusalem one way, and down the Kidron valley past Abu Dis and on to the Judean hills the other way.

Read Psalm 88 and Philippians 2.1–11 today. Then pause and think about the lifestyle of Jesus and pray for those going through times of pain.

# Tuesday: Learn to do good, search for justice

Jesus proclaims the Reign of God which brings hope to the oppressed, comforts the grief-stricken, feeds the hungry and restores rights to the defenceless, as the Scriptures promised . . . Though God's Reign is near, the disciples cannot sit idly waiting for its arrival – they must practise its values now, even if this seems impossibly naive and foolish in the present world. (Peter West, *Good News for Money? Poverty and Wealth in the Gospels*, 2003)

## *Back to the Shepherds' Fields*

From the viewing platform at St Peter in Gallicantu, if you turn away from Jerusalem and look in the opposite direction you are looking to Bethlehem and Beit Sahour. In our visit to the Christian town of Beit Sahour we were welcomed by the mayor, Fuad Kokaly. He talked about life in and around the Shepherds' Fields; in his words there is a challenge to us to respond and 'practise justice':

'The Israelis are confiscating more and more land, increasing the settlements, making roads so the settlers can move easily from one settlement to another, all the time squeezing the Palestinian community. This is why the Palestinians are afraid that finally we will find a Palestinian State that's 40 per cent of the West Bank and Gaza. They have the power, and the support of the international community, which means America. Are they ready to end the occupation? If they are then we can negotiate.

'We have a problem because sources of water are on the

West Bank but they are used by the settlers, they are controlling the water – and so they will determine how they could share the water with us. The equation must change. They should treat us as equal; we have the needs and the rights that the Israelis have.'

Mayor Fuad told me that the population of Beit Sahour is 14,000, and that 93 families have recently left. The last time I spoke to him, he said the Israelis were particularly targeting Christian areas. Was this still the case? 'Yes, this is an Israeli policy; they don't want Christians, because the Christians have the links with the West and they don't want that. They alone want to have links with the West. They are squeezing Beit Sahour so we won't have land to build – there is an Israeli military camp in the eastern part, and in the northern part a buffer zone and the wall, and we don't have land, so there is a kind of voluntary transfer, voluntary emigration. They don't come and take people and send them out, like 1948, but it leads to the same thing. So people are emigrating because they are seeking a better life. They want to work, they want to feel free, they want to have their dignity, and this is not allowed in these circumstances.

'But the Christians are still living here. They should continue their role and their message in our community. Christianity in Palestine has the message of peace, the message of love. So I think it is the Church's duty to save Christianity in Palestine, to keep it and to support it, and I think this is for the benefit of Christians all over the world. In 1948, 98 per cent of the people in Bethlehem were Christians; now in Bethlehem they are just 35 per cent. We in Beit Sahour are still the majority, 80 per cent are Christians – please support us.'

As we learn to do good and search for justice it requires

action on our part. Pentecost reminds us that we are not alone on the journey, we have the resources of God's Spirit; and Trinity teaches us something about the character of God that is our example and our motivation.

## Wednesday: 'Maybe someday we'll all be like you'

Psalm 19.14
Let the words of my mouth and the meditation of my heart be acceptable to you, O LORD, my rock and my redeemer.

### Jewish voices

#### Rabbi Jeremy Milgrom and military service

'I didn't insist on not serving, I just wanted to serve without a gun. The last time I was called in to serve was after I'd already written to the higher-ups saying I don't accept the moral authority; and they said, "OK, just serve this one more time and then we'll have a meeting." At that meeting they asked if I would be OK if they didn't call me to serve any more. I was worried this was a trap, and they just wanted to say, "Oh, it's not that you have ideals, you're just lazy and you don't want to serve your country, and sacrifice"! So I said, "Up until last year I would have been crushed by this decision, but now I can deal with it"! Inside, I was jumping for joy.

'And when I went to sign out, I went to this officer in my unit, and he said, "Congratulations! We won't meet again in uniform, but I wish you good luck in the rest of your life. And maybe someday we'll all be like you." I was so moved by that. And I said, "That's such a nice thing to say; how come you haven't been very helpful over the last five years, when I've tried to have something to do in the army that wasn't with a gun?" And he said, "Well, the problem was we couldn't find the right form to fill out for you." It's true – they don't have a form for people like me. They have a form for people with back trouble, and people who have domestic problems, or economic problems, but they don't have a form for someone who doesn't want to hold a gun for reasons of conscience.'

## Susan Barhoum: Teaching the children not to hate

'I try to teach my children that this is our homeland, and that their grandfathers grew up in this land, and this is where they belong. But though this land has been taken away from them they mustn't hate the Jews or the Israelis – though they may not like what they do. In October 2000 my son was only five years old; he saw what was happening on TV – the young men being shot, especially in the Galilee – and he would say, "I don't want to go to the mall (which is a Jewish shopping centre) because that's where the Jews are and they kill Palestinians, and I don't want to be killed." And this was a five-year-old. Nobody had said anything to him, but that was his reaction to what he was seeing. The children also ask about their grandfather's story; he was a refugee in 1948 and spoke a little to them about it before he died, but they were still too young to understand. Now they're becoming older, they want to understand what happened; it's part of their history, part of their lives.'

Susan spoke with pain about the killings in Nazareth in

October 2000: 'Police reacted so violently to the pro-
testers, and even people who weren't protesting, but were
just watching, were shot and killed. Thirteen died, and
hundreds were injured.' Susan went on, 'It's sad and it
angers me that things like this can happen and that people
can keep silent.'

## The environment, pollution and research

Susan works as Director of the Program Development
Department of the Galilee Society, a Palestinian health and
environment NGO and research institution: 'We do environmental justice work; where there are environmental
hazards in Israel, such as stone quarries and dumping
sites, a lot of them are situated next to Arab villages. We
are working with a coalition of different environmental
groups, who've been able to close several stone quarries.
In villages in close proximity to stone quarries 50 per cent
more children suffer from asthma as a result. Also we are
currently working against an incinerator in Shefa'Amr.
There's a big entrepreneur who's bought a piece of land in
Shefa'Amr for a waste incinerator. It'll be working 24
hours a day, with about 300 trucks a day bringing rubbish
to be dumped into the incinerator. The gases emitted from
the incinerator include dioxins, which are very poisonous
and could cause cancer. The site will be one of the biggest
waste sites in Israel, and waste will be coming from all
over Israel. The chimney will be so high you'll see it for
miles around, and the effect, they say, will reach Jordan
when the wind is in that direction.

'Last year, we were able to close an asbestos dump,
which was the only waste dump for asbestos in Israel and
it was next to an Arab village. It wasn't even according to
waste dumping standards, because it wasn't fenced in, so

for the children from the village this was an open space where they used to play, and there were a lot of cancer incidences. This was Sheikh Danoun, near Kafr Yasif. Asbestos is supposed to be buried in the ground, and they were pouring it on the surface. We were able to close down that site and now they are trying to clean it up.'

## Thursday: The alternative power of Pentecost

Mark 9.33–36

Then they came to Capernaum; and when he was in the house he asked them, 'What were you arguing about on the way?' But they were silent, for on the way they had argued with one another about who was the greatest. He sat down, called the twelve, and said to them, 'Whoever wants to be first must be last of all and servant of all.' Then he took a little child and put it among them; and taking it in his arms, he said to them, 'Whoever welcomes one such child . . . welcomes me . . .'

Our passage today is again set in Capernaum, with a very human incident with the disciples arguing who should be the greatest. Jesus reminds them to be a servant and like a little child – indeed, the first must be last. This is very typical of the teaching of Jesus, a reminder to reject the ways of domination and the misuse of power and status. This is the alternative power of Pentecost – the power to serve.

Today Bishop Riah talks of the steadfast vocation of

the Galilee Christians; I was chatting with him in the compound of St George's Cathedral in Jerusalem – actually on the roof!

'The Church up in Nazareth and Galilee is vibrant; it's different from here – people seem to be more settled, and some of them have emigrated and come back, when they discovered that living in the Diaspora is no fun. The numbers are increasing because of birth rates, but there are some Russians, of Christian background, who are using our churches for services, or holding their services in Upper Nazareth, led by Orthodox priests.

'So it's a different story altogether in the Galilee, partly because people did not leave their home towns; Nazareth people stayed there, Shefa'Amr people stayed there, Reineh people stayed there, Cana of Galilee people stayed there – people stayed in those villages and towns because they were meant to be part of Palestine, according to the Partition Plan of 1947.

'Also, the Church in Galilee is less troubled about status compared to Jerusalem. Status kills the spirit of fellowship in the way some in the hierarchy behave, disregarding others or underestimating how much others can do. This is not the case in the Galilee; there is a closer relationship among the Christian communities in places like Nazareth – it is an ecumenical community. In Nazareth we continue to have a week of prayer for Christian Unity; in Reineh all Christians celebrate Christmas together and all Christians celebrate Easter together; the same in Cana, the same in other villages. You can't think of celebrating Easter together here, even when Easter happens to come the same day; people wonder what's going to happen in the Church of the Resurrection, because of this business of status.

'The Christian community in Galilee is also viewed as a

131

serving community; we have a number of schools – in Nazareth there are ten high schools, with thousands of students. The good service rendered to the community at large, as with the hospitals and the clinics in town, gains respect.'

## Friday: Villages of Galilee

Amos 8.4–6
Hear this, you that trample on the needy, and bring to ruin the poor of the land ... buying the poor for silver and the needy for a pair of sandals ...

Susan Barhoum, whom we have met a couple of times before, introduced us to Dahoud Bader of the Association for the Defence of the Rights of the Displaced Persons. He explained their work and gave us some of the history as to why their work is necessary.

'The Association works for the defence of the internally displaced, those who have been displaced from their villages but are still within Israel. We are part of the Palestinian refugee population who were kicked out in 1948. As a refugee population we constitute 25 per cent of the Arab population in Israel, and as refugees we are also under the UN constitution that was passed in 1948, with the right of return which is UN Resolution 194.

'During and after 1948, many people were forced to leave; the Israeli army would enter the village and kill, either mass killings or just a few people in the village, to scare the rest of the village into leaving. This happened during 1948, but also following 1948.

'Over 400 villages were destroyed and their people were forced to leave. The internally displaced in Israel are about 250,000, and they go back to between 70 and 80 different villages that have been destroyed.

'In March 1948 there was an agreement between the villagers of el-Ghabsiya and the Israeli army that the army would not enter the village. But on 21 May the Israeli army entered the village, and the person who went up into the minaret carrying a white flag, as a sign of peace, was shot by the army and killed. Many of the villagers went back to their homes afterwards, but were kicked out again by the army. It led to many refugees writing letters asking for mercy from the Israeli government, to say that "we haven't done anything against the law, we're good citizens, allow us to return to our villages and cultivate our lands, we're peaceful people". All the requests were turned down.

'The two villages of Ikrit and Ba'aram went to the Israeli Supreme Court, and the Court ruled that they could return – that was in July 1951, and to this day they haven't been able to return, although they have a court decision. In September 1951 the community of el-Ghabsiya returned, but the Israeli military police arrested many of them and they spent several months in jail. Others were fined huge amounts of money for returning to their homes. They went to the Supreme Court, and at the end of November 1951 they also got a court ruling allowing them to return to their village. On 8 December the villagers returned but the Israeli army stopped them, saying that it was a closed military zone, and so the people cannot return, even though they had court decisions. It was an Israeli court, and even the Israeli military police were in contempt of their own court.

'In the Oslo peace process, the internally displaced within Israel found they were never mentioned. The Association is a network of different communities from villages trying to raise awareness. The issue for refugees within Israel is that many live within metres or kilometres of their own villages, and yet they can't go back to them. The refugees are also citizens of Israel, and of course Israel is proud to say that it is a democratic country. Democracy in our eyes means equality, and equality means getting back the right that we lost in 1948.'

We had told Dahoud that later that day Samuel Barhoum was taking us to an old village called al-Bassa, so he told us a little about it.

## The village of al-Bassa

'Al-Bassa was a very beautiful village, just below the mountains bordering Lebanon; it lies close to the coast. The population in the village was 3,500. You'll see in the village the ruins of three churches, as well as a mosque and the home of the priest. This village also had a college. The village was composed of Christians and Muslims, with about two-thirds Christian and one-third Muslim.'

Later I went to al-Bassa with Samuel. It is now an Israeli industrial area; the churches and the mosque have been used to keep animals, though these have now been removed, and the Greek Catholic church is locked. There is an old Presbyterian centre and clinic, and we saw soldiers going in there with their guns on some sort of exercise. The land is beautiful and rolls down to the sea. Samuel told me that people from Bassa who were baptized in the church are not allowed to worship there or renovate it: 'for them it is a disaster'.

## Saturday: Unrecognized village

1 John 3.16–18
We know love by this, that he laid down his life for us – and we ought to lay down our lives for one another. How does God's love abide in anyone who has the world's goods and sees a brother or sister in need and yet refuses help?

A bizarre feature of Israel is that there are over 100 unrecognized villages, which are villages that the government will not acknowledge, so they have absolutely no facilities and live in total poverty. Shehadeh Shehadeh talked about the villages in Galilee and also in the Negev, where he had just been:

'Two weeks ago I was in and around Beersheba, trying to see the situation of the Bedouin villages which are not recognized. There are more than 100 villages that are not recognized by the State of Israel; for them they don't exist, and the state does not give them any services at all – no water, no roads, no schools, even health services are almost completely absent in these villages. Their situation is terrible – very hard. I can't imagine how people could live in such a situation: trying to add another room to a tin house – and you know the weather in the Negev is very hot during the summer and very cold during the winter. They are succeeding in getting recognition for certain villages. Recently there was recognition of five villages in the Negev. The unrecognized villages in the Galilee are mostly Bedouins, and they are like the Bedouins in the Negev.'

I mentioned that I had visited the village of Ein Hod, and Shehadeh commented: 'Yes, the village is still there; the original village is still there, but Jewish artists live in it. The original people have been moved, by force, to hills not far away, and live in a village that is also tin homes. Recently they got water – but the children have to walk several kilometres to go to school. I think Ein Hod is going to be recognized; I hope so.

'In Galilee these villages do not exist for the government. They are not on the map. They have no electricity, no services of any kind; the least you can get as a human being is not found in those villages.

'In the mind of many Western people the State of Israel is *the* democratic state within the Middle East, but the history of the State of Israel since its creation in 1948 has nothing to do with justice or equality or democracy. They do not treat people as equal human beings, but like animals. I am sorry to say that but this is the situation, I can't ignore it.'

## Holy rage

Helen Steven, in *Jesus – Way of Peace* (Christian Aid/ Hodder, 2003) is grappling with the incident in the temple in John 2.16, where Jesus says 'to those who sold doves, "Take these things out of here! Stop making my father's house into a marketplace!"' She quotes South African Allan Boesak writing of 'a holy rage', saying it is 'the ability to rage when justice lies prostrate on the streets and when the lie rages across the face of the earth. A holy anger about the things that are wrong in the world . . . To rage at the senseless killing of so many and against the madness of militarism. To rage at the lie that calls the threat of death and the strategy of destruction "peace".'

It is time for action; there is 'naught for your comfort' here and we must find ways to express concerns, to protest against those things that are wrong, and to have some 'holy rage' about those who are forgotten. Sometimes in our worship we need a chance for people to express the anger they may feel at the injustice in our world. It is almost like a moment of therapy before we can go forward to a more positive hopeful and healing response. Part of our worship is to 'challenge the powers', to challenge the power of false gods, to open our eyes to where we have put our faith in 'golden calves'. And as we see in Jesus the defeating of the power of death, we see that life is restored to its rightful place, the abundant life of which Jesus spoke.

So worship should be about restoring the right understanding of our world, the right balance. It is rejecting domination of one group over another – we can cling to tribal gods no longer; the living God calls us to constantly reassess our views in the light of the values of God's reign, and then it is time for living out these values in action.

## The living God

> You're the one, you're the living one
> You're the truth against the false
> You're the friend of the poor
> And you tear down the walls
> You are the living God.
>
> You break the walls of hatred
> Of prejudice and greed.

You heal the broken hearted
Restore the ones in need.
You're power to the powerless
And hope to the weak
You are the Prince of Peace.

You're the one, you're the living one . . .

You're not like the god of money
You're not like the god of war.
You were born into a stable
You live beside the poor.
The price is not all that matters to you
People mean so much more.

You're the one, you're the living one . . .

So teach us to be like you, Lord,
And tear false idols down,
To bring the light of the gospel
Wherever the dark is found.
Your kingdom brings hope to a world torn apart
May we show your love today.

(Words and music Garth Hewitt © Chain of Love Music)

## Sunday: Trinity – we believe in a communal God

John 14.15–16
If you love me, you will keep my commandments.
And I will ask the Father and he will give you another
Advocate, to be with you for ever.

138

So we arrive at Trinity Sunday, having travelled from Easter, from Jerusalem, on a search for St George, past the Shepherds' Fields where we saw 'naught for your comfort', on up to Nazareth and different parts of Galilee, and back to Jerusalem for Ascension and Pentecost. With Trinity we come to the question of God and the character of God that we need to understand, as knowing something about the character of God shows us how to live, and also helps us to recognize the danger signs when something is wrong.

Our passage for today is one that shows the close link between Jesus, the Father and the Advocate or Spirit. Trinity is a doctrine of deduction from passages such as this which helped the Church address the fact that God is one yet in some way is reflected in three 'persons' or 'faces', as Archimandrite Philotheos said. Another passage that shows this close proximity is Ephesians 5.18–20: 'but be filled with the Spirit, as you sing psalms and hymns and spiritual songs among yourselves . . . giving thanks to God the Father at all times and for everything in the name of our Lord Jesus Christ'.

Once again, let's ask one of our Galilee Christians, Fuad Dagher, for some thoughts on this: 'We believe in a communal God. We believe in a Trinitarian God. We believe in a God who is able to live with himself – the three images, Father, Son and the Holy Spirit. We see this as a direct message of how we are to live, the principle of community because we believe in a communal God. After all, we live in a small village called the world, and we are citizens of the same village, of the same world, and we have to learn how to live in this community, to live in communion with each other, since God is a God of communion, a communal God, in the Holy Trinity.

'Yes – we have to make it clear that the kingdom of God

starts here on earth. It's what we are doing now, we are building towards the kingdom of God, towards this community, towards this communal life as it is shown in the Trinitarian God. Therefore I think we have to make this earth a better place in which to live. We have to make a piece of heaven on earth, because for me hell or heaven is not a place, it is a state I live in – it's a way of living. We are called to build towards this earthly kingdom of heaven, and make our planet a better place in which to live.'

This means resisting what is wrong and saying 'yes' to the ways of peace. The clarion call that Bishop Trevor Huddleston gave in the 1950s about apartheid in South Africa needs to be echoed once again. Racism, discrimination, a wall of separation, all are a reality in the Holy Land – there is 'naught for your comfort . . . the sky grows darker yet . . .' The sky does look very dark, but people of the Resurrection community know that the darkest hour is just before dawn. Our task is to keep heading towards the dawn, and to help hasten the day when Palestinian and Jew can link arms together and say, 'At last the dawn is here.' On our journey we have travelled in the company of the Christians of Galilee and Bethlehem who have shown us something of the character of God at these significant times of the year; we have also heard from Jewish and Muslim voices of hope, peace and justice. They have all shown that there is a way forward towards the dawn if we are courageous, non-violent, active and just, and do unto others as we would have them do to us.

## Prayer

O Holy Trinity, God of community, open our eyes to your ways, open our hearts to your love, and open our minds to your attitude, where all are invited and all are welcomed and where the healing hope of the Easter gospel becomes a reality. As we are challenged by the Ascension to 'do something', may we make the ways of God visible in our world, walking away from the excluding views of the past, strengthened by the Spirit of Pentecost to live and work to bring your peace. Amen.

# ⊛⊕⊛ amos trust

justice and hope for the forgotten

Come and meet the 'living stones' with Garth and Gill Hewitt and the Amos Trust. Make the journey to Galilee, Jerusalem and Bethlehem. For more information on Amos pilgrimages, contact the Amos Trust (details below).

Garth Hewitt's books are by kind permission of Amos books.

For more information on the work of the Amos Trust, on Garth Hewitt's talks and concerts or to buy copies of Garth's previous books (*Pilgrims and Peacemakers* and *A Candle of Hope*) and his CD *Journeys: The Holy Land*, please contact:

> Amos Trust
> All Hallows on the Wall
> 83 London Wall
> London EC2M 5ND
>
> Telephone: 020 7588 2638
> Fax: 020 7588 2663
> Email: info@amostrust.org
> Website: www.amostrust.org
>
> (registered charity number 292592)

Garth Hewitt's songs are published by Chain of Love Music/administered by Daybreak Music Ltd, PO Box 2848, Eastbourne BN20 7XP.